Sociology from the Ground Up: An Examination of Life in the Lower Tiers of American Sociology

Stan C. Weeber, Editor

ISBN:1463520867
ISBN-13:9781463520867

DEDICATION

This book is dedicated to the many mentors who have assisted me over the years in the Midwest and in the South, USA, and in the United Kingdom.

CONTENTS

ACKNOWLEDGMENTS

I would like to thank the librarians at Frazar Memorial Library at McNeese State University for their kindness and competence in assisting me with locating some of the research materials for this book, especially for Chapter 1. The Inter-Library Loan Department has been very helpful over the years in helping me find those particularly hard-to-find items. I could not have produced this book without their support. I also wish to thank co-authors Daniel Rodeheaver (Chapter 4) and Carol Campbell (Chapter 5) for their intense loyalty and support over the years. Without them, this book could not have ever been produced.

1 SOCIOLOGY'S ACADEMIC CASTE SYSTEM

In sociological circles during the 1990s, there was much negative talk about the future of sociology. This was a "Gloom and Doom" decade where troublesome projections were being made about the viability of sociology as an academic enterprise in American universities.[1] Actually, these writers were continuing a number of earlier discussions about what direction or directions sociology should take both theoretically and empirically.[2]

In the litany of sociological woes that reverberated through sociology departments of the 1990s in books and sociological publications, departmental closings, declining enrollments, and loss of academic prestige were major sources of alarm. But there was more, much more:

> Sociology professors often lack enthusiasm for their subject matter, which is reflected in boring class presentations and dull textbooks. In addition, issues of race and gender are rarely integrated into Sociology textbooks or into course curricula, alienating students of color and further marginalizing them from the educational process. Finally, many sociology departments fail to offer courses in the core areas of the discipline, focusing instead on narrowly specialized areas like ethnomethodology or drug and alcohol abuse.

> Because of the current economic climate, students and parents have become utilitarian consumers who view education simply as a means to employment. Contemporary sociological questions may not appeal to students who have little desire to question American institutions and to promote social change. In addition, the undergraduate major in sociology is not perceived as one that leads to professional job opportunities, and many people do not know exactly what sociology is. For students who do not want to continue on to graduate school, there is little economic incentive to major in sociology. Very few sociology departments prepare students for careers in applied research. Finally, the creation of separate criminology and social work departments has led to fragmentation and loss of student majors as well as the loss of specific career paths.[3]

This long critique alone is plenty damning. Of all the problems identified, the economic problems were among the aspects of the crisis that were the most devastating to sociology as a developing science. Administrators often ranked sociology as a poor contributor to the economic functioning of the university or college – as was the case at Washington University in 1989 – while mathematics, science, and technology were being perceived as being more lucrative for the university's bottom line and more pragmatic for students. Sociology, additionally, was not seen as being integrally linked to any program of economic importance to the university, whereas subjects like political science, which is often linked to pre-law programs, and economics, which is often tied to business schools, could enjoy the benefits of "riding the coattails" of more lucrative academic subjects.[4]

Though catastrophe was avoided, the negative talk of the Nineties was damaging for all who lived through it. In retrospect, it was the splintering of sociology's self confidence and the collective labor pains of the dislodging of the huge sociological mass from its elite core. The gloom and doom rhetoric was essentially the mourning of the loss of the kind of respected sociology that had been practiced in the Golden Era of sociology in the '40s and the '50s, and for a brief period beyond that. This is the tradition that today's sociological elite hopes to emulate. In contrast, a much different "mass" sociology pursues more applied projects and does so in relative anonymity when compared with the elite. These are the two sociologies of American sociology, and they are separate and unequal.

Elite Sociology

In the narrow stratum at the top of sociology's stratification system are the scholars of the elite schools that dominate the discipline in several ways. The department names are well known: Chicago, Wisconsin, Cal-Berkeley, Michigan, and UCLA head the list. These schools have regularly appeared at the top, or near it, in the sociology department rankings over the years and the remainder are in the top 25 of the 1995 Academy Press rankings.[5] In general, these upper ranked departments are the older departments with the best reputations, having the largest and most visible faculties and largest rosters of highly qualified graduate students. Research is the priority here, and the schools of which they are a part are large enough and rich enough to fund quality research centers where proposals can be honed and high-quality research carried out. They teach the core areas of the discipline, and especially within these areas, the trendy "small theories" and fashionable advanced quantitative methods that are used in the top sociology journals.[6]

One of the many ways that this stratum exercises and displays its dominance is through the numerous departmental rankings that have been published over the years. Though what constitutes quality is always debated and is highly controversial, there is a tendency for the top schools to come out on top, regardless of the method used in calculating quality.[7] This suggests, then, that among multiple raters there is a rough consensus of sorts about which departments are the best. Table 1 presents the ranking of sociology departments from a 1995 study, along with that school's tier ranking (the rating of the institution as a whole) in the 2004 *U.S. News and World Report* survey. There is a fairly high correlation between the two: the correlation coefficient is +0.69.

Second, the elite stratum dominates the publications in the major journals, both in articles published and in the domination of the editorial boards of the top journals. This has been an obvious fact to even the most casual observers of sociology, but visual evidence of this appears in Table 2. This presentation is a combination of data from two snapshots of publications and editorial staffs of the three top journals in the field in 2001 and 2004. The data indicate that the sociological elite rule the publication game, although there are some unexpected results in the data. Over 50 percent of the authors are from Tier 1 schools and over 80 percent are either Tier 1 or Tier 2 authors. There is some appearance of a limited amount of egalitarianism in that about 19 percent of the authors come from Tiers 3 and 4.

A better picture emerges from the unaggregated data in Table 3. From this table we can see that in the schools that placed in the top four places in terms of number of authors representing their schools (Michigan is the last of these schools), Tier 1 schools made up 29.7 percent of these authors. At this point there is a difference of only 7.3 percent when one subtracts the figures in column 5 from those in column 4. In other words, all but 7.3 percent of the authors are from Tier 1, which suggests a relatively high concentration of authors of Tier 1 schools in the top four places, as expected.

Looking at the schools that placed in the top 8 places overall (Washington State is the last of these schools, alphabetically arranged), about 45 percent were Tier 1 authors, and overall, the top 8 places made up just over 60 percent of all the authors. Here there is a separation of about 15 percentage points.

At the bottom of the distribution there are several schools tied for 12th or last place, all with one author each being published in an elite journal. At the very bottom of this list, at the final school tied for last place, there is about a 30 percent separation between all authors regardless of Tier, and the percentage of Tier 1 authors. Taken as a whole, the table suggests a heavy concentration of Tier 1 authors in the upper ranks, or stated another way, Tier 1 authors were published with a much greater frequency than were authors from the other tiers. This, of course, is something that we would have expected prior to the data analysis. Some hope is extended to faculty at the lower ranked schools that they can be published, although their publications will be infrequent when compared with faculty from the elite schools.

Third, the elite consume their own graduates. I do not mean that they literally hire their own graduates, as this practice was essentially outlawed long ago. However, the elite schools do hire many young faculty who have recently graduated from other elite schools. Thus, there is a kind of inbreeding that perpetuates the elite. Baldi found that the most distinguished of sociology departments place an overwhelming majority of their graduates who get jobs in Ph.D.-granting departments rated as distinguished or strong, while departments at the bottom of the prestige hierarchy are unable to place their few Ph.D.- department bound graduates in other categories than their own.[8] Moreover, there is a noticeable pattern of downward mobility for the low prestige departments that has become more pronounced over the years. Baldi found that while a handful of graduates from low prestige departments were once able to find jobs in high prestige departments, this phenomenon has virtually disappeared today. No graduate between 1985 and 1992 who obtained a Ph.D. from a department rated "good" or lower was able to land a first job in a "distinguished" department. Furthermore, across all prestige groups, no one moved up more than one prestige category during 1985-1992.[9]

In a 2004 paper Burris updated research on departmental stratification and outlined a new way to conceptualize the differences between the various prestige layers. First, he notes once again the highly stratified nature of American sociology and the limits of social mobility: the top five ranked Sociology departments hire 56 percent of their new hires from other top five percent schools, and 91 percent from the top twenty schools. Upward mobility was severely restricted as only 9 percent of graduates from the lesser ranked schools (those below the twentieth rank) made it into a job at one of the elite five schools. The mobility barrier appeared to be especially strong at the "top 20" level. That is, graduates from the bottom 74 Ph.D. granting schools were most likely to be rebuffed when seeking employment in the top 20 schools. Interestingly, Burris found the barrier between the top five and the remaining 15 of the top 20 schools was not as strong.[10] Given this rigid academic caste system, Burris concurred with

Caplow and McGee who observed long ago that a young scholar's initial choice of a graduate school sets an indelible mark on a student's career that is unlikely to be overcome by the post-graduate achievement of even the most brilliant scholar.[11] In addition, what is being shared and interchanged in the various prestige layers is "social capital," a term that is typically used to describe rich veins of civic participation. As applied here, it refers to networks of association and social exchange that tie together the most prestigious departments.

By suggesting that there is an elite of Tier 1 schools and a "mass" sociology consisting primarily of the Tier 3 and Tier 4 schools, this leaves an awkward question about Tier 2 in the *U.S. News* rankings. What are we to make of these schools? I think that they are a detached, floating kind of group that is more like Tier 1 than the masses. They have bridges upward and may take advantage of them. Surely they try, though publications, to publish their way into the elite by building their resumes and then trying to secure an elite position. That is one way to get there, and as we've already observed, the elite journals publish a fair amount of articles from Tier 2 schools (see Table 2). Securing an editorial board assignment in one of the top journals may be another pathway. Still another

Table 1. Sociology Departmental Rankings (1995) and School Institutional Ranking (2004).*

School	1995 Rank	1995 Tier	2004 Rank	2004 Tier
University of Chicago	1	1	13	1
University of Wisconsin-Madison	2	1	32	1
University of California-Berkeley	3	1	21	1
University of Michigan	4	1	25	1

Continuation of Table 1:				
School	**1995 Rank**	**1995 Tier**	**2004 Rank**	**2004 Tier**
University of California-Los Angeles	5	1	26	1
University of North Carolina-Chapel Hill	6	1	29	1
Harvard University	7	1	1	1
Stanford University	8	1	5	1
Northwestern University	9	1	11	1
University of Washington	10	1	45	1
University of Pennsylvania	11	1	5	1
Indiana University	12	1	67	2
Princeton University	13	1	1	1
University of Arizona	14	1	99	2
Columbia University	15	1	11	1
University of Texas-Austin	16	1	53	2
John Hopkins University	17	1	14	1

Continuation of Table 1:				
School	**1995 Rank**	**1995 Tier**	**2004 Rank**	**2004 Tier**
Pennsylvania State University	18	1	48	1
Yale University	19	1	3	1
Duke University	20	1	5	1
New York University	21	1	35	1
University of California-San Diego	22	1	32	1
University of California-Santa Barbara	23	1	45	1
University of Minnesota	24	1	60	2
SUNY – Stony Brook	25	1	117	2
Ohio State University	26	2	60	2
Vanderbilt University	27	2	19	1
University of California-Riverside	28	2	84	2
University of Illinois	29	2	40	1
SUNY – Albany	30	2	123	2
Rutgers University	31	2	60	2

Continuation of Table 1:				
School	**1995 Rank**	**1995 Tier**	**2004 Rank**	**2004 Tier**
Washington State University	32	2	99	2
University of Maryland	33	2	53	2
SUNY-Binghamton	34	2	78	2
Cornell University	35	2	78	2
Florida State University	36	2	112	2
City University of New York	37	2	---	2
Brown University	38	2	17	1
University of Massachusetts	39	2	91	2
University of Southern California	40	2	30	1
University of Iowa	41	2	57	2
Michigan State University	42	2	73	2
University of Florida	43	2	48	1
Boston University	44	2	64	1
University of Illinois-Chicago	45	2	---	3

Continuation of Table 1:				
School	**1995 Rank**	**1995 Tier**	**2004 Rank**	**2004 Tier**
University of Notre Dame	46	2	19	1
University of Virginia	47	2	21	1
University of Georgia	48	2	58	2
University of Connecticut	49	2	64	2
University of California-San Francisco	50	2	117	2
Texas A&M University	51	3	67	2
Purdue University	52	3	58	2
University of California-Santa Cruz	53	3	67	2
University of Kentucky	54	3	107	2
Boston College	55	3	40	1
University of Oregon	56	3	123	2
University of Colorado	57	3	78	2
Syracuse University	58	3	55	2
University of Pittsburgh	59	3	67	2
Brandeis University	60	3	32	1

Continuation of Table 1:				
School	**1995 Rank**	**1995 Tier**	**2004 Rank**	**2004 Tier**
University of Missouri-Columbia	63	3	73	2
North Carolina State University	64	3	84	2
Louisiana State University	65	3	---	3
University of Kansas	66	3	95	2
University of Nebraska	67	3	107	2
Loyola University-Chicago	68	3	99	2
University of Delaware	69	3	67	2
University of New Hampshire	70	3	95	2
Northeastern University	71	3	---	3
Tulane University	72	3	44	1
Arizona State University	73	3	---	3
SUNY – Buffalo	74	3	---	3
Bowling Green State University	75	3	---	3

Continuation of Table 1:				
School	**1995 Rank**	**1995 Tier**	**2004 Rank**	**2004 Tier**
University of Hawaii-Manoa	77	4	---	3
Southern Illinois University	78	4	---	4
University of Tennessee	79	4	95	2
American University	80	4	99	2
Colorado State University	81	4	112	2
Fordham University	82	4	84	2
University of Utah	83	4	117	2
University of Akron	84	4	---	4
Western Michigan University	85	4	---	3
Mississippi State University	86	4	---	3
University of Cincinnati	87	4	---	3
Kent State University	88	4	---	4
University of Oklahoma	89	4	117	2
University of Denver	90	4	87	2

Continuation of Table 1:				
School	**1995 Rank**	**1995 Tier**	**2004 Rank**	**2004 Tier**
Catholic University of America	92	4	112	2
Georgia State University	94	4	---	4
Oklahoma State University	95	4	---	3

* The 1995 Tier level rank is from the *Academy Press* rankings of that year. Ranks 1-25 = Tier 1; Ranks 26-50 = Tier 2; Ranks 51-75 = Tier 3; Ranks 76-95 = Tier 4. The 2004 ranking and tier level is from *U.S. News and World Report.*[12] The Pearson's Correlation Coefficient for different tier assessment systems is +0.69.

way to get hired by an elite school is to secure a postdoctoral fellowship at the school and to build up social capital with the faculty there.[13]

Mass Sociology

The massive group of departments not in the elite is alive and productive, though at the same time financially strapped and struggling. You can find them in Tiers 3 and 4 of the *U.S. News* rankings or in the bottom half of the 1995 ratings of top Ph.D. granting departments. Texas A&M, Purdue, Bowling Green State University, Howard University, Georgia State University, and Oklahoma State University are among the schools on this list. If the list has a "southern" flavor, it is because schools in the South are more highly represented in this group as Table 4 suggests. This large group of departments is responsible for the teaching and training of thousands of undergraduates who use sociological training as a stepping stone to jobs in the private and public sectors, or as a first step in achieving a graduate education in the discipline. It is a primary vehicle for students gaining an appreciation of other cultures, for learning to think sociologically, and for gaining a small measure of what C. Wright Mills called the sociological imagination. Most of the heavy lifting in this regard is done in these lower ranked teaching institutions, where more emphasis is placed on effective teaching than scholarly research and research output. Because some of these schools are larger than the elite schools, teachers there face larger workloads, bigger classes, and longer hours spent on teaching duties. Like any other job performed for the masses (and not for a select few), it is underappreciated and an endeavor that people know little about. And though teaching is emphasized in mass sociology, it is not the only item on the agenda of the average working sociologist. Lower-tiered sociologists must also show some proclivity for publication and research, and they must engage in public service. These are the three areas emphasized by the American Association of University Professors as being important elements of life in academia.

The split in the discipline, though painful, has resulted in a sociology that is far different than the salad days of the 1940s and 1950s, when sociology enjoyed a kind of golden era. Though the elite effectively control most of the financial resources of sociology, sociology, as practiced on a day-to-day basis in American colleges, is mostly now a sociology by and for the masses. It is a kind of sociology that would have caused the great elite sociologists of the past to be greatly disappointed in what their life's work has become. In mass sociology there are no people of the stature of Daniel Bell, Talcott, Parsons, or Robert Merton: people of substance who had ideas about the society in which they lived and offered cogent analyses of substantive current events and controversies. With the possible exception of Robert Putnam, sociology is now largely devoid of such people. In this sense, "old-school" sociology did die with the passing of Riesman, Coser and other great ones.[14] Now, it is composed of a sea of autonomous but relatively anonymous people pursing narrow specializations which – though more quantitative and

Table 2. Percentage of Papers Authored and/or Edited in Elite Journals in 2001 and 2004, by Tier

Tier	Percent authored	Percent edited	Combined, Authored and Edited
Tier 1	56.0 (51)	76.8 (275)	72.8 (329)
Tier 2	25.3 (23)	19.0 (68)	20.1 (91)
Tier 3	11.0 (10)	2.5 (9)	4.2 (19)
Tier 4	7.7 (7)	1.7 (6)	2.9 (13)
Total	100.0 (91)	100.0 (358)	100.0 (452)

scientific and sophisticated than ever before – are simultaneously more distanced from public discourse and from public understanding.

Mass sociology was something that had to evolve because early sociology was so successful. Early on, the few people graduating with Ph.D.s in sociology could find jobs easily. In these halcyon days the elite schools provided the graduates for just about all the sociology departments nationwide. In this period, the *American Journal of Sociology* documented every graduate and even listed their dissertation title. Soon, the deluge of graduates proved to be so great that this practice could not be continued. And as sociology proliferated, not everyone could teach at an elite school. Excess people with Ph.D. credentials needed to go somewhere. Out of necessity, they went downward. The supply of new graduates exceeded the demand of universities that would hire them. In the Seventies we began to see and hear of the crisis related to this, sometimes called the 'Blue Collar Blues." Highly educated sociologists who could not find teaching jobs were working as blue collar laborers or as taxi drivers to support their families.[15] In this context, the proliferation of specialties that were so bemoaned as "fragmentation" or "sub-field drift" proved to be the savior of many a young sociologist. Specialization was good for sociology in that it gave the surplus of sociologists something to do. They could teach and still do research in their specialization, could win awards and publish articles and become journal editors, and with those fruits could get tenure and be promoted. Without specialization, none of this would have been possible. Viewed in this way, sociology was both a beneficiary and a victim of its own early successes and excesses.

The influence of specialization can be seen by comparing the top and bottom of sociology in Table 5. Here we compare the course offerings and the types of courses that are taught at the top ranked school, the University of Chicago, and the lowest ranked of the doctoral granting schools, Oklahoma State University. Chicago offers more courses at the advanced undergraduate level and at the graduate level. Their faculty is over twice that of Oklahoma State,

Table 3. Authorship of Papers Published in Elite Journals, 2001 and 2004, by School, Rank, Number of Authors, and Tier.

School and Rank	Number of Authors (N=288)	Tier	Cumulative Percentage of all authors	Cumulative Percent of Tier 1 authors
1. (tie) Ohio State	12	2	4.2	---
1. (tie) Stanford	12	1	8.4	4.2
1. (tie) Wisconsin	12	1	12.6	8.4
2. Penn State	11	1	16.4	12.6
3. (tie) Cal-Berkeley	10	1	19.9	16.1
3. (tie) Chicago	10	1	23.4	19.6
3. (tie) Indiana	10	2	26.9	---
3. (tie) Princeton	10	1	30.4	23.1

Table 3 Continued: School and Rank	Number of Authors (N=288)	Tier	Cumulative Percentage of all authors	Cumulative Percent of Tier 1 authors
3. (tie) Washington	10	1	33.9	26.6
4.Michigan	9	1	37.0	29.7
5. (tie) Arizona	8	2	39.8	---
5. (tie) North Carolina	8	1	42.6	32.5
6. (tie) Cornell	7	1	45.0	34.9
6. (tie) Duke	7	1	47.4	37.3
7. (tie) Iowa	6	1	49.5	39.4
7. (tie) UCLA	6	1	51.6	41.5
8. (tie) Columbia	5	1	53.3	43.2
8. (tie) Indiana U. of PA	5	3	55.0	---
8. (tie) Penn	5	1	56.7	44.9
8. (tie) SUNY, Albany	5	2	58.4	---
8. (tie) Washington State	5	2	60.1	---
9. (tie) Brigham Young	4	2	61.5	---
9. (tie) California-Davis	4	1	62.9	46.3
9. (tie) California-Irvine	4	1	64.3	47.7

Table 3 Continued: School and Rank	Number of Authors (N=288)	Tier	Cumulative Percentage of all authors	Cumulative Percent of Tier 1 authors
9. (tie) Harvard	4	1	65.7	49.1
9. (tie) Johns Hopkins	4	1	67.1	50.5
9. (tie) Maryland	4	1	68.5	51.9
9. (tie) Minnesota	4	1	69.9	53.3
9. (tie) Texas	4	1	71.3	54.7
10. (tie) Akron	3	4	72.3	---
10. (tie) Northwestern	3	1	73.3	55.7
10. (tie) Western Washington U.	3	1	74.3	56.7
11. (tie) California-San Diego	2	1	75.0	57.4
11. (tie) MIT	2	1	75.7	58.1
11. (tie) Missouri-St. Louis	2	4	76.4	---
11. (tie) Mississippi State	2	3	77.1	---
11. (tie) Mount Holyoke	2	1	77.8	58.8
11. (tie) Nebraska	2	2	78.5	---

Table 3 Continued: School and Rank	Number of Authors (N=288)	Tier	Cumulative Percentage of all authors	Cumulative Percent of Tier 1 authors
11. (tie) New York University	2	1	79.2	59.5
11. (tie) North Carolina State	2	2	79.9	---
11. (tie) Notre Dame	2	1	80.6	60.2
11 (tie) Oregon	2	2	81.3	---
11. (tie) Rutgers	2	1	82.0	60.9
11 (tie) U. of Houston	2	4	82.7	---
11. (tie) Wisconsin-Milwaukee	2	3	83.4	---
11. (tie) Southern California	2	1	84.1	61.6
12. (tie) Boston College	1	1	84.4	61.9
12. (tie) Boston U.	1	2	84.7	---
12. (tie) Brown U.	1	1	85.0	62.3
12. (tie) California-Riverside	1	2	85.3	---
12. (tie) California-Santa Barbara	1	1	85.6	62.5

Table 3 Continued: School and Rank	Number of Authors (N=288)	Tier	Cumulative Percentage of all authors	Cumulative Percent of Tier 1 authors
12. (tie) Cal-State, Long Beach	1	2	85.9	---
12. (tie) Cal-State, Los Angeles	1	3	86.2	---
12. (tie) Carnegie Mellon	1	1	86.5	62.8
12. (tie) Catholic U. of America	1	2	86.8	---
12. (tie) City University of New York	1	2	87.1	---
12. (tie) Clarkson U.	1	2	87.4	---
12. (tie) College of Charleston	1	1	87.7	63.1
12. (tie) Colorado	1	2	88	---
12. (tie) Dartmouth	1	1	88.3	63.4
12. (tie) Emory	1	1	88.6	63.7
12. (tie) Florida	1	1	88.9	64
12. (tie) Florida Atlantic	1	4	89.2	---

Table 3, Continued: School and Rank	Number of Authors (N=288)	Tier	Cumulative Percentage of all authors	Cumulative Percent of Tier 1 authors
12. (tie) Florida State	1	2	89.5	---
12. (tie) George Washington University	1	1	89.8	64.3
12. (tie) Illinois	1	1	90.1	64.6
12. (tie) Louisiana State	1	3	90.4	---
12. (tie) Maine	1	3	90.7	---
12. (tie) Missouri	1	2	91.0	---
12. (tie) New Mexico	1	3	91.3	---
12. (tie) New School for Social Research	1	3	91.6	---
12. (tie) Northeastern U.	1	3	91.9	---
12. (tie) North Texas	1	4	92.9	---
12. (tie) Oberlin College	1	1	93.2	64.9
12. (tie) Philadelphia University	1	2	93.5	---

Table 3, Continued: School and Rank	Number of Authors (N=288)	Tier	Cumulative Percentage of all authors	Cumulative Percent of Tier 1 authors
12. (tie) Reed College	1	1	93.8	65.2
12. (tie) Rice	1	1	94.1	65.5
12. (tie) Santa Clara	1	1	94.4	65.8
12. (tie) Skidmore College	1	1	94.7	66.1
12. (tie) Southern Illinois	1	4	95.0	66.4
12. (tie) Southern Maine	1	3	95.3	---
12. (tie) Southern Methodist	1	2	95.6	---
12. (tie) SUNY, Stony Brook	1	2	95.9	---
12. (tie) Tulane	1	1	96.2	66.7
12. (tie) U. of Massachusetts	1	2	96.5	---
12. (tie) University of Memphis	1	4	96.8	---
12. (tie) Vanderbilt	1	1	97.1	67.0
12. (tie) Virginia	1	1	97.4	67.3

Table 3, Continued: School and Rank	Number of Authors (N=288)	Tier	Cumulative Percentage of all authors	Cumulative Percent of Tier 1 authors
12. (tie) Washington-St. Louis	1	1	97.7	67.6
12. (tie) Wisconsin-Whitewater	1	2	98.0	---
12. (tie) Yale	1	1	98.3*	67.9

*totals do not equal 100 due to rounding.

Table 4. Schools in 2004 *U.S. News* Rankings, by Tier and Region

	Tier 1	Tier 2	Tier 3	Tier 4
	# %	# %	# %	# %
East	11 (44.0)	11 (44.0)	10 (40.0)	4 (21.0)
West	7 (28.0)	4 (16.0)	4 (16.0)	5 (26.3)
Midwest	6 (24.0)	6 (24.0)	7 (28.0)	5 (26.3)
South	1 (4.0)	4 (16.0)	4 (16.0)	5 (26.3)

so the classes are smaller. Perhaps more important than the number of courses taught there is the quality of the courses. The core areas of the discipline are covered, and within these core classes, the latest theories are presented and debated. Then, there is the huge advantage in the quality of the research seminars. Chicago offers more statistical classes and more with the most recently used statistical methods. Oklahoma State has fewer offerings at the undergraduate and graduate level, larger classes, and a tendency to favor applied sociology over theoretical sociology. Additionally, the methods classes are broader, survey types of classes.

Once the division between elite and mass had occurred, the problems within "mass" sociology escalated - with many parallels to the process that occurs when people slip into poverty and thus become more vulnerable to a bevy of social problems. How could these inferior beings keep up with the elite or hope to join it someday? When teaching four classes per semester and advising a substantial number of students, and balancing expectations of reasonable amounts of public service, a rigorous research agenda is not possible unless one attempts to shatter world records for sleep deprivation or amphetamine use. Nor does the school generally have a quality research center where proposals can be developed and critiqued. Even the travel budgets required to travel to do research or to present research findings at professional meetings (at the lower levels this is typically the far less prestigious regional and state meetings) are very limited, and are evaporating as I speak. Moreover, faculty in the teaching institutions do not have access to the kinds of doctoral courses being taught in the important core areas of the disciplines at the big schools, nor knowledge of the kinds of small theories that are developed and tested in those areas. Absent as well is the knowledge of the trendy methods and model building that tend to go along with the small theories. If you are a Ph.D. graduate of an elite school you know these things, but if not, you do not know them. Overall, what's being generated and shared by the big schools are exchange networks that are rich veins of social capital. And the Marxian "sinking into misery" of the bottom tiers was suggested long ago by Merton who called this the Matthew effect:

> For unto every one that hath shall be given, and he shall have abundance: but from him that hath not shall be taken away even that which he hath.[16]

Talcott Parsons also saw the future and it was not good:

> ... a man who works in a university research setting early in his career has opportunities to accumulate a research record which, in competition for the higher level university

appointments, cannot be matched by the man who has carried a heavy load of undergraduate teaching in an atmosphere where little research is going on – although their capabilities may be equal. There is, therefore, a tendency to make the college teacher a kind of second class citizen of the profession's academic branch.[17]

Table 5. A Comparison of Sociology Course Offerings for Advanced Undergraduates and Graduates at the University of Chicago and Oklahoma State University, Fall 2004 Semester

	Chicago	Oklahoma State
Total Courses Offered		
Advanced Undergrad	44	36
Graduate	92	40
Courses Common to Both Schools		
Advanced Undergrad	Social Research Methods Sociological Theory Urban Sociology Population Studies Sociology of the Family Social Movements	Social Research Methods Sociological Theory Urban Sociology Population Studies Sociology of the Family Social Movements

Graduate	Quantitative Methods Sociology of Education Social Movements Organizational Sociology Contemporary Theory	Quantitative Methods Sociology of Education Social Movements Organizational Sociology Contemporary Theory
Courses Unique to Each School (Partial List) Advanced Undergrad	 Social Structure & Change Statistical Methods of Research Organizational Analysis Social Change Urban Structure and Process	 Rural Sociology Sociology of Death and Dying Applied Sociology Clinical Sociology Juvenile Corrections and Treatment Sociology of Agriculture
Graduate	Social Change Organizational Analysis Political Sociology Institution of Education	Gender and Work Environmental Sociology Medical Sociology Organizational Deviance

Table 6. Overall Rankings for Top 15 Elite Teaching Colleges in Total Pages and Total Articles Published in High Impact and ASA Journals Listed by Sociological Abstracts, 1960-1999.*

School	Overall Rank	Mean Rank	Rank for Total Pages	Rank for Total Articles
Connecticut College	1	1.5	2	1
Oberlin College	2	2	1	3
Wellesley College	3	2.5	3	2
Bryn Mawr College	4	3.5	4	3
Smith College	5	5.5	6	5
Skidmore College	6	6	5	7
Hobart and William Smith Colleges	7	7	9	5
Barnard College	8	7.5	7	8
Wesleyan University	9	8.5	8	9
Dickinson College	10	11	10	12
Williams College	11	11.5	14	9
Middlebury College	12	12.5	10	15
DePauw University	13	13.5	12	15

School	Overall Rank	Mean Rank	Rank for Total Pages	Rank for Total Articles
Gustavus Adolphus College	14	14	13	15
Trinity College	15 (tie)	14.5	14	15
Holy Cross College	15 (tie)	14.5	20	9

*Adapted from *The American Sociologist*, Fall, 2001.[18]

There are two more groups relevant to the discussion that could well be overlooked, one that is part of the elite and one that is part of mass sociology. The elite that I'm talking about are the elite teaching institutions. These are the Tier 1 Liberal Arts and Comprehensive Colleges in the *U.S. News* rankings that are known for their excellence in teaching. The teachers there have managed to avoid the second class status predicted by Parsons. These institutions are selective in their student populations, provide rigorous training for their students, and also do a surprising amount of high quality research and publishing. In this latter regard, they are no match for the elite Research I (to use the Carnegie language) schools such as Princeton, Harvard, Yale, and Wisconsin. However, they do compete among themselves to see which department can do the most publishing. As Table 6 indicates, Connecticut College, Oberlin, Wellesley, Bryn Mawr and Smith head the list. The picture here is clear: these are small, private colleges with large endowments funded by wealthy alumni. The schools have a long tradition of excellent teaching, small classes, and an academic reputation fueled by occasional publications in very high caliber journals.

At the bottom of the heap, so low as not to be ranked, is what arguably could be called the unseen Tier 5: the junior colleges. Despite doing a huge amount of the introductory sociology teaching of students that will later attend a Tier 3 or 4 school, the sociologists in this bottom caste are the all but forgotten "undocumented" workers of sociology. They may have five classes to teach instead of the three to four that is the norm in Tiers 3 and 4. They are likely to be without doctorates, serving as part time adjuncts while working on their dissertations or trying to pass their comprehensive exams. They are among the lowest paid workers in sociology. In some cases, they are Ph.Ds who could not land a university tenure track job in what has been, periodically, a very congested job market. This may be especially the case for those sociologists who are not mobile and who are restricted to working in a specific geographic area. Some of these sociologists give up on their dream of tenure track jobs, and become permanent temporary workers.[19] They are good teachers, as a teaching demonstration is almost always required as part of the job interview process. They are probably more likely to use technology in the classroom than their more highly ranked peers in Tiers 3 and 4, and are generally expected to make the material "come alive," a task that any teacher of social theory knows is difficult. Moreover, they are closely monitored, with special attention to the teaching product being produced.[20] These sociologists generally labor hard under the most trying of conditions, and talk about a thankless job: their large contributions in motivating and shaping the lives of the largely diverse populations they serve go mostly unnoticed and unappreciated.

To sum up this section: what is being detailed here is a caste system of professional sociology. The Tier 1 schools are at the top (both the elite research and the elite teaching schools), and the Tier 2 schools are detached from the elite but still longing to be elite. They have more in common with the elite than with the mass. The massive group of sociologists in Tiers 3-4 are in the teaching institutions; and below that, there is a figurative "undocumented caste" called Tier 5, comprised of junior college and technical school sociologists that do a lot of sociology's dirty work and heavy lifting.

Structural Changes in University Life

The situation described above with respect to sociology has not developed within a vacuum. Studies of the stratification of other disciplines in academe show similar levels of prestige stratification. Burris effectively demonstrated that the caste-like nature of current academic sociology is a condition shared by several social science disciplines, and if he is correct, critical social networks of collegial association are shared among the elite as a treasured resource among the elite departments in several social science disciplines. Stated another way, sociology is not alone in its caste-like stratification system.[21]

What further separates the rich and poor of academic sociology – in fact the rich and poor of any discipline, is the growing gap in resources and the ability of the best schools to restrict themselves to the best students while the remainder must deal with the diverse masses. As such, the stratification of the academic world resembles the stratification of America and the world in general, and it is in a much larger social context that we must look to get a bigger picture of what has happened to sociology.

The changes within sociology are couched within a larger series of structural changes that transformed college life from one of idyllic imagery to one of hard blue-collar realities. The images of college as lawns, trees, period buildings, and privileged, upscale students carrying books across quadrangles still lives on at the elite schools, but for the mass the situation is much different now. As John Flower, former president of Cleveland State University reflected upon a long career in academe, he clearly captured the reality of higher education today. With respect to today's students:

> There is no limit to their human diversity. They include welfare mothers who take their babies to class with them, men and women in the eighth and ninth decades of their lives still wanting to learn, released prisoners struggling to acquire the skills that will enable them to get along in society, and throngs of workers intent on improving themselves.[22]

What he's referring to is the kind of student that appears in what he calls the "downstairs" of academe that is occupied by the vast millions of college students today. This downstairs, I contend, is essentially the same as the Tiers 3 and 4 of the *U.S. News* system, and the bottom half of the schools in the 1995 sociology rankings. Flower's own school is in Tier 4, so his opinion carries some weight. For this downstairs category of school, training in skills and crafts to obtain jobs in changing marketplaces is what the important task of a college education is all about. Flower contrasts this with the elite and exclusive "upstairs" of economic and socially privileged students who attend the topmost private and flagship state institutions that possess billions of dollars in endowments. Here, the important matter of education is educating in ideas and concepts in order to improve minds and hopefully to improve morality and character as well. These elite schools, because of their money, are less susceptible to the sweeping changes that have occurred in higher education. They in many ways separated from public higher education. The worlds are so different that Flower suggests that we speak of "higher educations" rather than higher education.[23] The two worlds are so rigidly separated that Flower would no doubt concur with the idea that there is a caste system in American higher education.

Public Sociology and the Future of Sociology

Today, sociology has found its niche in the academic world, though not the one envisioned by the founders of the field or the contemporary sociologists who guided sociology through its golden era. Sociology has settled in at many schools as an important provider of diversity and cultural education, and at others, it is a popular social science requirement and alternative to psychology. It has been welcomed as a training ground for diversity and for cultural sensitivity; and, it provides the student a wider view of the world than the one they may have been raised with.

Meanwhile, the American Sociological Association continues to work on its tarnished image, with an emphasis on the public role of sociologists and the production of knowledge that benefits society.[24] This is a role that the lower tiers of sociology are well suited for. The effort, however, is plagued by the same sort of criticism and sniping that was characteristic of the Nineties, and part of the long critical tradition of sociology in general.[25] This latest effort to unite sociology appears doomed to failure despite the best intention of the sociologists who created and promoted this public vision. The two sociologies cannot be united.

What is the future of sociology? I contend that sociology is just now coming to grips with the nature of the "problems" within the discipline. It is finally realizing that it is a caste system. Underlying this system is a massive amount of structural inequality of which sociology is simply a microcosm of what is going on in academe in general and in America and the world. The future gives no hope that this situation is going to change except for the fact that the current situation will only get worse, that is, the enriching of the top stratum and the "enpooring" of the masses along with the continuing depletion of social capital between the elite and the mass. This means that it is more important than ever for young scholars to contemplate their initial choice of graduate education, for it is likely to be the entry into a caste from which they will not be able to escape, even if they are the brightest and most efficient student in the world. It is important for the lower ranked schools to realize that they are going to have to help themselves, because no one else is going to do anything for them. An effort by some elite schools to reach out to some of the four year "teaching colleges" ended up a disaster.[26] In spite of the best idealistic intentions at the outset of the project, there was only a minimal or token desire to share trade secrets with the masses, and the mass schools had few resources available to help themselves by attending the meetings. Hence, hardly any valuable strains of social capital were being developed by the mass schools by participating in this program.

The future may also help us finally come to grips with the sociology rating games and exactly how they work. Because much emphasis is put on the reputation of the school in determining its rank, it stands to reason that people filling out the rating instrument at the top ranked schools know nothing about the lower ranked schools, have little association with them, and have little networking or sharing of that important commodity, social capital. The response rates for the instruments are less than exemplary, and it would be interesting to know the Tier level of the people returning the ratings to *U.S._News*. Despite all the controversies about ratings, the *U.S. News* rating system will continue to be important, if for no other reason than the fact that it gives a complete stratification system for U.S. schools and one that is generally compatible with the sociology department ratings. Moreover, it is a general guide to the young sociology scholar in the choice of schools, and that choice becomes more important as the boundaries between castes become more rigid.

I am both pessimistic and optimistic about the future of sociology. I have deep pessimism about the future of the regional associations. I fear that as their resources are "enpoored," they will go the route of some of the state associations and simply cease to exist. As travel budgets shrink, faculty will have to pay their own way to the regionals. This in turn will cause them to rethink the strategy of reading papers at regional meetings prior to publication in order to get comments for future revisions. Based upon my own experience, many are simply bypassing the meetings, and sending their best relatively un-critiqued drafts to the journals, hoping for a "revise and resubmit" response. The situation reminds me of the farm crisis of the '80s, when smaller farms either went bankrupt or merged with larger farms. Innovation may be the key here: on line conferencing may be one of a number of ideas on the table to help save the regional associations.

I am optimistic, however, about the national association. It is reaching out to its diverse publics in an aggressive attempt to educate the public about what sociology is, its role in the academic world, and the uses to which sociological knowledge may be applied. This is long overdue. If introductory sociology students are sometimes mystified by what sociology is, consider what the public or publics at large must think of us. The ASA research department, despite its critics, has produced data that indicates the present and future viability of sociology in academe.

Plan of the Book

I want this book to serve as a time capsule concerning what sociologists do at the lower tiers of American sociology. Sociologists are familiar enough with the elite; this book is about sociology's "mass." Relatively little has been written about these lower-ranked teaching institutions, and there have been very few works highlighting how sociology looks from the perspective of sociologists teaching at these institutions. Accordingly, this book is a snapshot and analysis of the field of sociology "from below," or "from the ground up," and shows how professional sociology is accomplished at some of the teaching institutions. This book will be of interest to sociologists working in, or training for, teaching jobs in the lower-tiered sociology schools. It is also a snapshot of what it was like to be a "working sociologist" in American universities in the late 20th and early 21st centuries.

I suppose there are not many that care what goes on in the lower tiers. But considering the large amount of training of U.S. sociology students taking place in those tiers, the book is an instrument for future lower tiered sociologists and students to gain an introduction to their life's work and what they may encounter. After an introduction to the big picture of the lower tiers in Chapter 2, subsequent chapters give the reader an entrée into the worlds of teaching, research, and public service. The final chapter emphasizes the positive aspects of working in the lower tiers.

2 'THE BIG PICTURE' IN THE LOWER TIERS – TEACHING, RESEARCH AND SERVICE

Upon hearing the phase, "teaching institution," one might conjure up mental images of professors spending long hours to prepare for class, even longer hours of teaching and grading exams, and an ongoing struggle to keep abreast of a constantly changing subject matter. To an extent, this is an accurate portrait of real life in teaching institutions, as teaching is the main emphasis there. A Dean of Liberal Arts who was administratively responsible for the teaching of sociology at one midsized teaching institution told me: "the clearest route to tenure at this school is a serious program of effective teaching."[27] Imagine, then, the nervousness of a raw young recruit newly hired to a teaching position in such an institution, when it's discovered that he or she must have a research agenda and also perform some university or community service functions. Teaching, research, and service are the three areas emphasized by AAUP, and serving in a primarily teaching institution brings no exemption from the three requirements. Realistically, if (s)he was property mentored at the doctoral level, (s)he should have seen this coming. Yet, as the reality of the requirement sinks in, the candidate may experience symptoms not unlike that when reading his graduate school's requirement for the dissertation. This chapter discusses this "big picture" that one faces in the sociology teaching institutions: the demands of teaching, research, and service.

Teaching

As teaching is the main function in the teaching institutions, being able to effectively teach and communicate ideas to others is a key skill that is vital to a person's survival. A skilled researcher at an upper tiered school whose teaching is terrible might be able to get by on his or her scholarly reputation. At the lower ranked schools, though, it is difficult to imagine such a poor teacher lasting long, even if his own personal circumstances dictated that he apply at one of the Tier 4 schools. Occasionally, candidates for teaching positions are asked to prepare a presentation and to present it before faculty and graduate students; the purpose of this process (among other things) is to weed out the poor communicators from the pool of available candidates.

If poor teachers are eliminated before they can get signed on, how then is teaching effectiveness measured for those good teachers or communicators who make the cut and get hired? Often, it is the formal and informal feedback of the students themselves: informally, word of good teaching may spread as students meet with advisors to schedule classes; and formally, the quantitative scores from the student's evaluation of the course at the end of the semester would probably be higher for the better teachers. And the two types of feedback should more or less correlate well for the more skilled teachers. The same teacher that causes a student to mutter to no one in particular in the hallway, "Gawd, that man cannot talk," is probably one that will have a low quantitative score at the end of the semester.

Other schools rely less on student feedback, understanding full well that the difficulty of the courses may have something to do with the student's perception of "good teaching." They may temper the high overall quantitative scores of some teachers by comparing their "course difficulty" scores, that is, the students' rating of how difficult a particular course was to them. If a teacher is considered good but is still difficult, this may be an important aspect that can impress some administrators. At this kind of school, the administration may look at the grade distribution of the teacher, to check if too many A's or B's are being given. They may expect, for example, that no more than 20 percent of the students will achieve a grade of A. This scenario might apply more often at the most upwardly mobile of the lower tiered schools. At still other schools, faculty may rate each others' teaching, although I've never figured out how that is supposed to work, unless that faculty member sits in on a colleague's class for an entire semester. More likely than not, the grade given to his colleague is the faculty member's impression of his colleague's teaching, gleaned from discussions with other faculty and with student advisees, or an examination of the faculty members' syllabi used in his/her courses.

George Ritzer is a critic of an approach to faculty evaluation that is too quantitative, fearing that it is one of many trends pointing toward the "McDonaldization" of collegiate education.[28] His biggest fear is that some kind of quantitative "template" for evaluating classroom instruction may float from school to school, or schools may otherwise start to copy each others' methods of evaluating teachers. Quantification has its advantages: simply relying on the students' quantitative evaluations of the professor is an attractive alternative for administrators because it is a numbers oriented and supposedly "objective" rating from the student/consumers themselves, and not subject to the administrative whim of the faculty supervisor that is evaluating a given faculty member. Ritzer objects vigorously, saying that such a rubric favors the teacher who is a "performer" rather than one who is a "thinker." Ritzer is convinced that performers score higher on the student evaluations because they are funnier, or make the subject matter more interesting, or are the least demanding of the professors. On the other hand, a "thinker" may be a very demanding professor who puts students through the difficult tasks of critical thinking. He or she just might be the best and most effective of the teachers at the school, and could still be not well liked by the students, and a poor performer on the student evaluations.[29]

Set against a quantitative approach is one at the other end of the spectrum with respect to statistics or numbers. It is usually completely devoid of quantitative methods, and essentially amounts to whether or not the employing supervisor "likes" the candidate and then "likes" the teaching product that he or she produces. I've never been able to figure out what this means exactly, and use of the term "likes" immediately makes me nervous. Because the term is so vague and nonspecific, it can mean just about anything, from how the professor dresses, or how much they smile, to how many pounds the person weighs, to the content of the course as reflected in the syllabus, or what other professors say about the professor being rated. The things that the supervisor "likes" about the professor may or may not be things that are highly correlated with effective teaching.[30]

Adding "degree of difficulty" points to the task of teaching at the teaching institutions is the diversity of the student body and its ever increasing utilitarianism as consumers of sociology. The curriculum needs to be diverse to make the subject inclusive and interesting to all; at the same time, a number of reasonable accommodations must be made to a population that is getting older and composed more than ever of non-traditional students. These people may work long hours and have extensive family obligations, in addition to attending school. With little time to spare, they may gravitate inevitably to the courses for which they can get the highest grade with the least amount of energy output. Critical evaluations of societal institutions may not be their cup of tea, as they hope to someday advance, based on their college education, in the same institutions that sociologists love to criticize.

Most students in the teaching institutions are diligent, hard-working, committed, and dedicating to graduating within a four to six year window. However, after 2000 I began to see with increasing frequency a type of student that was strangely familiar, but at the same time "new." I call this student the pseudo-student.

The pseudo-student is utilitarian in the extreme, dedicated only to advancing with reasonable progress (to keep the financial aid coming), and is busy with other things - so much so that, to be painfully blunt, school is not a real high priority. The "other things" may be intercollegiate or intramural sports, family obligations, divorce, change of living arrangements and/or moving to a new place, work obligations, recreation (such as hunting or fishing), entertainment, or any number of activities that rate higher than school on the student's list of priorities. This is the kind of student that is likely to be absent for much of the semester save for the key days when test reviews are given, or the test days themselves. They are also the first to inquire about their final grades, often well before they are due at the registrar, and may do so with such annoying repetition that the professor either acquiesces, or simply takes his or her work home. They are also the first to protest, rather vehemently, if they feel wronged by their final grade. Despite being absent for weeks during the regular semester, the pseudo-student is one that can be seen stalking the campus during the semester breaks, trying to track down the professor who "shafted" them, despite the professor being gone on a well deserved vacation. The absence of the professor is uniquely annoying to the pseudo, who may complain to the professor's superiors, or may even call the professor at home to voice their disappointment.

Some of my colleagues attribute this pseudo-student to a digitally entertained generation that does not want to be bothered with the onerous and disinteresting tasks of attending lectures and taking notes, and who would just like to stay home or stay in their offices and complete school there. Yet, this pseudo student phenomenon is something I had seen before and after much reflection, I discovered where I had seen it.

In the late Sixties and early Seventies, the pseudo-student of that generation was in school simply to avoid being drafted and sent to war in the rice fields of Southeast Asia. Partying, alcohol, illicit drug use, sex, and political protest were the most important things to this student. School was not a priority. He was interested in academic progress only so much as it related to staying off probation and in school, and avoiding the potential glare of the local draft board. Academically bright but classically underachieving, this student was a painful annoyance that often wore his countercultural political ideology on his sleeve in full public view, even being disruptive in the classroom at times to make a political point.

I disagree with the elitist view that these students were psychologically sick individuals that were, as one critic exclaimed, working out unresolved emotional conflicts with their parents in the university setting.[31] The easiest thing for a powerful person to do is to declare all the "different" people mentally ill. I believe, on the contrary, that these students were in full command of their mental processes, had the chutzpah to question the status quo – to actually use Mills' sociological imagination - and that was exactly why they were so infuriating to the professors of the Vietnam Era.

Today's pseudo, though possibly conflicted by depression, schizophrenia, or a variety of diagnosed or undiagnosed mental illnesses, is armed with medicines that can be used to control these illnesses. These students are stable enough to function generally well in the community, and so for the most part they are in full command of their mental processes. And that is why they are so infuriating to their Millennium Era professors. Reason suggests that these students should learn to prioritize their life; but alas they have, and academics are at the bottom of the list. There is probably nothing worse than someone who does not want to achieve anything more in the college classroom than a passing grade.

The thread that links the two generations of pseudo-students is this: a complete and overriding preoccupation with themselves. The Sixties generation was saving themselves from possible death in Vietnam whereas the Millennial generation is saving itself from the realities of having to work hard for something in order to achieve it. They want everything and they want it now, with convenience and with little effort. That includes their college degree.

The impression so far may be that teaching sociology in a teaching institution is a negative experience. Let me say that overall the positives outweigh the negatives, and overwhelmingly so. The pseudo-student is somewhat rare statistically, although it seems that there is at least one such student per semester that is the proverbial thorn in the side, and the pain of that thorn gets my attention. I've had semesters that I looked forward to the end of the lectures, mostly because of a difficult pseudo. Most of the students, though, are committed people who enjoy college and especially value a professor that is good at what he or she does. It is for these kinds of students that the professor stays in the game.

The most vulnerable period for a teaching faculty member is at the beginning of their careers, when their teaching may get the most scrutiny from superiors. It is at this period that poor teachers or teachers who are poorly evaluated tend to get weeded out from the better performers. Yet, some of the decisions made about these young, powerless faculty are somewhat arbitrary, and reflective of the growing consumerism on college campuses. While finishing up his dissertation at a Tier 4 school, a colleague of mine came across the following set of circumstances and relayed them on to me.

A Teaching Fellow in sociology, who had been known to my colleague's department – quite favorably I might add - for several years as a Master's student and candidate, Master's graduate, doctoral student, Teaching Assistant, and then Teaching Fellow, was let go after what had been reported to be one "very bad semester" of teaching. The original source of the "bad teaching" allegation had not come from students' quantitative evaluation of the instructor, but from what was said during an appointment made by a disgruntled student to an Assistant Dean of Student Services. The student was a sub 2.0 GPA who was not doing well in the class. The allegation was that the instructor was showing an excessive number of films in the class (a class in social stratification as I recall), the films were from a Marxist perspective, and that nothing of any value was being transmitted to the students. The Assistant Dean promised to investigate thoroughly.

My friend and colleague happened to be an employee of the same Assistant Dean at the time. He was finishing up his dissertation, and though working hard in his job, he was basically marking time until his graduation. To her credit, the Dean sought him out and interviewed him, as he knew the Teaching Fellow fairly well. He urged caution and leniency based upon the TF's prior record, which had been exemplary as far as he could ascertain from speaking with faculty in the department. He indicated that there could be personal problems involved the TFs performance but that he did not have any facts relevant to that at all. He left the interview with the Dean feeling that whatever came of the investigation, that fairness would reign. The Fellow in question even called my friend, fearful that she would lose her job. He simply reported to her what he knew about the case at the time, and tried to be as positive as he could be, given the circumstances.

Later, the department came down hard on the Teaching Fellow. She was let go at the end of the semester that was "poor teaching" in the eyes of the student complainer, and was not allowed to teach again at the school as far as my colleague could tell. A factor in the rapid end of her career at the school might have been the presence of a new department head who might have been unaware of her prior accomplishments. After being fired, her teaching career continued at two other schools that she has served, one of them a Tier 2 school and the other being a junior college, where the quality of teaching is supposedly monitored more closely than it is in the university setting. Her firing must have been a personal setback that discouraged progress on her degree; in 2011 she has still not graduated with her doctorate and has run up against time limits for completion of the degree.

Obviously, TFs are vulnerable and have little protection, and far less protection than the tenured professor has against the "bad semester" phenomenon described above. A few schools have unionized their teaching fellows, but this is the exception and not the rule. Teaching fellows come and go; student feedback via evaluations and reports to advisors, rather than direct observation of teaching, is often the cause of their staying or leaving. But the above episode appears to be harsh, even in the era of the new consumerism. Students, it would appear, have the capacity to fire a Teaching Fellow based upon a single complaint.

Lest professors be lulled into the belief that this new consumerism is going to go away, all they have to do is examine the extent to which technology is being pushed into the curricula of the university setting. I attended a training session in 1994 on Powerpoint presentations. At the time such technology was relatively new, and the presenter made the basic point that "the age of the sage on the stage" was basically dead. The message was that the curricula needs to be both relevant and interesting to the student.

Despite the drawbacks, the job of teaching in the lower tiers, if done well, can be a very secure one. True, there are no bright marquee lights in Tier 4, and at times the structural problems such as the budget woes can be overwhelming. However, employment is mostly secure, and you can be grateful for the problems you've left behind.

For example, gone are the days of adjunct work, when one student not appearing to register for your class as promised means that your class may not make its minimum enrollment, and you might have to work in a warehouse or do landscaping in the awful hot summers of the South.

Gone is the pressure of having to live up to the very high expectations that you would have to meet in the upper tiers. As one department head at a Tier 4 school told me, in relation to a newly hired professor who had recently escaped a Tier 2 school: "she's so glad to get away from that pressure of bringing in that all that external grant money…. Here, she can just concentrate on teaching, which is what she wanted to do in the first place …"[32]

With tenure, gone is the pressure of having to prove yourself.

You've already proven that you can do the job, and now you just have to maintain that, to show some consistency. Even at schools where there is post-tenure review, the earning of tenure brings with it a basic sense of security and belonging. Post-tenure review may require no more than maintaining an average level of competency when compared with one's departmental peers.

Gone is the pressure of having to move your family to a new place, where social relationships must be started anew. As one faculty member who settled in at a Tier 4 school told me: "I had opportunities to leave, but my family enjoys it here … why root them up and take them out of a good routine, something that they like …."[33]

Research

Research, as I routinely tell my introductory sociology students, is the difficult part of sociology. The behavioral models being constructed are complicated and mathematically sophisticated, and are getting more accurate in terms of explaining behavior; and, research requires that for every lofty concept you are interested in studying, you have to measure it somehow and in a way that others, namely your sociological peers, generally approve.

That being the case, the newly recruited Ph.D. who interviews at a teaching institution might be nervous when encountering the publication requirement of the department because it involves the hardest part of his future work. However, if the school is serious about making the new hire welcome, or they are desperate for some reason to fill the position, they just might make an effort to downplay the requirement. One demonstrably nervous recruit was told by a reassuring Dean in one of his interviews: "We're not going to work you like a dog for six years and then fire you, like they do at the big schools – taking all of your publications and glory for themselves. That's exploitation. We don't do that here."[34] Relieved, the recruit signed on at the school.

At other schools, the bar may be set so low with respect to publications that the requirement itself almost disappears – as I discovered at one school in 2005. A friend's brilliant though occasionally annoying colleague from graduate school had gone through the gauntlet of the academic world after graduation, from assistant professor to full professor, in just eight years – a grand accomplishment indeed. He had mostly ridden the wave of his excellent teaching, and that made up for a mediocre publication performance. His publications amounted to three workbooks or study guides that accompanied a well known sociology textbook.[35]

A full professor at a college in southeast Texas, in evaluating the publication record of an assistant professor up for tenure, said that "his (the candidate's) publication record is so weak that you could almost use it to write a parody of the requirement."[36] The candidate still managed to get through the tenure gauntlet based upon other academic strengths besides research.

Nor were these the only instances that I encountered: at one school in the Deep South, the newly appointed sociology department head had no publications at all, and had risen to the top with a combination of innovative teaching methods, strong committee work, and a cozy relationship with the Dean. At a school in central Texas, the long time graduate theory professor and difficult grader of theory doctoral comprehensives had only one publication to his credit, but he advanced to full professor based on his tough but fair teaching style, and for being a challenging and effective teacher.[37]

At the other end of the spectrum, I have heard of Tier 3 and Tier 4 schools that want to advance up the food chain of the academic world of sociology, and correspondingly put some pretty hefty publication requirements upon new recruits. An acquaintance who applied for a sociological theory teaching job at a Tier 3 college in central Texas was told that he would have to crank out four theory publications per year for six years in order to make it through the gauntlet and become tenured. The publications needed to be in high quality journals.[38] If this was a ploy to discourage the applicant, it worked: the potential recruit declined the position.

Real life at many teaching institutions may be somewhere in the middle of the extremes I suggested; that is, the requirements are neither too high nor too low, and reasonableness reigns. Further, there is some resistance to constructing requirements that are absolutely quantitative with little room for flexibility. Researchers who interviewed sociology department heads found a range of ways to approach the research requirement, all reasonable:

> We certainly will never define general expectations for scholarly productivity simply in terms of numbers of books and published articles.
>
> I don't think we would agree on any specific numbers – importance of papers and books would determine how many, I think.
>
> We look at where the articles or book was published – citation of the book and reviews. A small list of publications in the ASR is as impressive as a large or a long list of publications in B and C journals or publishers.[39]

Interestingly, the researchers found that the higher up the scale of schools in terms of their scholarly productivity, the less likely it was that there would be any kind of quantitative expectation. It appeared that a preoccupation with numeric requirements was more on the mind of the department heads at the lower-productivity schools, presumably also the lowest-ranked schools.[40]

A problem faced in Tier 4, and probably part of the explanation for the generally low level of research productivity in the tier, is the problem of name recognition. Suppose that you do try to break the mold and publish in respectable, high-quality journals, your name and that of your school often mean nothing to the journal editors who evaluate your manuscripts as they come in to the journal. Having built up little or no social capital with scholars outside of your own tier, the editor doesn't know you at all in the typical case; and he may wonder where this little school is, and who is this person, anyway? A perfunctory reading of portions of the submitted text is often enough for the editor to decide that the manuscript is not worthy of publication. The most honest of editors will ship your paper back to you without having sent it out for review; this happened to me once.[41] Other editors play games with your mind, sending the paper for review without any intention of it being published. I've never known for sure, but widely suspected that what more likely happens in such cases is for the journal to cash your submission fee, and then route the "unpublishable" paper to a bulldog of a referee who has a long history of rejecting manuscripts.

The journal keeps the submission fee, rejects many papers, and with the high rejection rate can rationalize the journal as being of "elite" quality. Not a bad way to fund your journal if you can make it work. I suspect this from my own personal experiences.

In the spring of 2004 I submitted a paper to a journal of political sociology based at an Illinois school. The editorial board consists of people I'd never heard of along with some big names in the field such as Richard Flacks, Ted Goertzel, Joseph Lopreato, Charles Moskos, Anthony Oberschall, Anthony Orum, Frances Fox Piven, Charles Tilly, and Michael Useem. The paper I submitted was about Shibutani's theory that news is improvised, or more likely to be based upon rumor, when there are conditions of high anxiety.[42] The theory has been used to explain the news coverage of the bombing of Pearl Harbor and the assassination of John F. Kennedy, and I thought it also might apply to the news coverage of the hunt for Osama Bin Laden in the fearful, tense post September 11 period.

The journal rejected my paper, which is fair enough. This happens occasionally, even to the most elite sociologists from time to time during the peer review process. I do have problems, though, with reviewers who have not kept up with the literature in their field, as the comments of Reviewer A suggest:

> What is the implication of tagging Shibtani (sic) a 'late' modernist. It is that he died last month? His study of rumor as collective problem solving is not a modernist tract but a classic example of participant-observation as practiced by the Chicago School.[43]

I found little humor in this glib remark, which spoke volumes about the reviewer and his lack of knowledge of recent sociological theory. When looked at from the standpoint of postmodernism, Shibutani's 1966 book about rumor processes in the making of news is near the end of modern period and close to the beginnings of postmodernism and its deconstruction of the ideas of the Enlightenment. In this sense it is late modernist. The reviewer went on to make five substantive suggestions for how to revise the paper that were more constructive, and I was grateful for these suggestions. But the tone of the review had been set by the opening shot referenced above, and I was inclined not to assign much weight to the reviewer's comments. Reviewer B also suggested rejection, and made many of the same substantive remarks as Reviewer A, only without the condescending language. Reviewer B's comments were such that even I was convinced that the paper was not ready for prime time, and needed a complete overhaul.

The reason I am relating this story, however, has to do with the decision of the editor to pick this particular set of reviewers. A sheet of comments followed the remarks of Reviewer A, and I'm quite sure the remarks were for the editor's eyes and not for the author's:

> I keep hoping that, some day you will send me a paper I won't have to reject. I feel bad every time I have to do this... In this case what strikes me as a paper by a still immature student needs to be fully rethought to be publishable. I am disinclined to subject us both to repeated reviews of poorly revised drafts. Better reject it outright and let the author know the kind of work that needs to go into an academically respectable paper.[44]

My suspicion that my work had been dubbed "student" work by the editor, and had thus been forwarded to the "bulldog" reviewer, were reinforced by these comments. In 2005, an international journal agreed to publish the paper.

Fearing that his manuscripts were getting such harsh but arbitrary handling by certain journals, a Tier 4 colleague of mine conducted an experiment. He had a friend at a northern Tier 1 school, and had worked on several projects with him. They decided to alternate the order of authors when sending papers to journals. Though authorship in reality was always equal, the coauthored papers got a better outcome at the journals when the northern author from Wisconsin was listed as the senior author. After that, my colleague tried whenever possible to coauthor papers with northern colleagues and was not afraid to allow them to be the senior author, even if their contribution to the paper was minimal.[45]

Even if the result with the publisher is good, I found one of the more annoying aspects of publishing today is the amount of time that it takes to get published. It can take 12-36 months, perhaps even longer, to get your paper to the journal, to have it reviewed, and then for the editors to send feedback on the portions that need to be revised. The problem, I believe, is that it is increasingly difficult for journal editors to find competent and reliable reviewers for their publications. For the young assistant professor bucking for tenure, it stands to reason that you had better have several manuscripts out there all at once. Trying to focus on one article at a time is poor time management and may cost you your job.

I suspect that some of the journals are under funded; the editors are overworked; and there is reliance upon student help whose sense of moral responsibility is not at its highest. This leads to delays that are unforgivable yet entirely human. Even in three situations where the end result was positive, unusual things happened.

The first serious paper I wrote as a doctoral candidate was submitted to a journal in Oklahoma that I am still very fond of to this day. I waited patiently for a response, not knowing how long it would take to get an answer. I was consumed with doctoral coursework, and with the responsibility of preparing my introductory level sociology classes that I taught as a Teaching Fellow. About a year later, I received a call from the editor. My paper had been misplaced, apparently by a student helper. It had been sent out for a review, but all the subsequent correspondence had been lost. The editor apologized profusely, and asked me to resubmit the paper so that the whole process could be started over. After much correspondence back and forth, and much revision, the paper was published in 1997, about two and a half years after originally being submitted.

A similar story can be told in 2004, this time about a journal based at a school in Michigan that has a fine reputation. The paper was submitted in April, 2004. Busy with multiple writing and teaching projects as an assistant professor, I again waited patiently, and just before the Christmas break of 2004, I wrote a short note to the editor asking for a progress report on the paper. The editor, highly embarrassed, had a note in his file that the reviews had been received and a decision rendered; yet there was no documentation at all: no paper, no reviewer comments – nothing. He agreed to start over again, this time with an accelerated review process. Apparently what happened, according to the editor, was that he was having difficulty finding reviewers who wanted to comment on the paper, a piece of specialty applied research dealing with the evaluation of an anti-smoking program targeting grade school students. This time, he asked us as authors to suggest some potential reviewers and we did so, with the qualification that we had not had any recent contact with any of them. We complied, and by March, 2005 we learned that our paper had been accepted for publication, subject to some minor revisions.

At times, the wait for a decision is just agonizing slow. A paper that my mentor Dan Rodeheaver and I sent to a high ranking journal based in Iowa was rejected the first time around, but the editors graciously allowed us to revise and resubmit it at a later date. Ultimately it was accepted, but the amount of time burned was an annoyance; we had even written the editor at one point, suggesting that we would withdraw the paper and take it elsewhere if there was no answer soon.[46]

In the Rodney Dangerfield world of Tier 4, book publishing is no easier a task than trying to get published in a journal. Again, the editors do not know you or even care who you are. The better mannered editors respond promptly with a rejection, and this is actually welcome as it ends the suspense quickly. Even if your work is accepted there may be problems, as I found out in the spring of 2004.

A national publisher with a good reputation agreed to publish a book on militias that I co-authored with Dan Rodeheaver. They promptly accepted our proposal and a date was established for our manuscript to arrive. Upon arrival, not much time elapsed before the editorial staff informed me of a few mistakes (mostly clerical and grammatical) that needed to be corrected. So far, so good, and we were delighted that the project was going forward and moving relatively quickly through their publication system.

In January of 2004, the processing of the book changed hands from the editorial staff to the sales and marketing staff, and with this transition I was introduced to a different type of corporate animal than I've ever seen before in the publishing business. As part of the contract that I signed, I had to deliver an order for 100 books before the actual printing of the book could begin. I was planning to use the book for one of my courses, so I arranged for my local university bookstore to place the order. It took some time for the order to go through due to staffing issues in the local bookstore. In the meantime, I began to receive messages that were almost like the "dunning" letters I receive to remind me that it's time to pay an overdue bill. Two messages from the publisher encouraged me to "fulfill my contract," which left me feeling like I was working for a local mafia of some kind, and not a university.[47]

In the meantime, my co-author was interested in seeing the book promoted on the publisher's website; he had lined up several universities that wanted to buy the book. However, the publisher balked at his request, as the order for the 100 books (the corporate requirement) had not yet been received. After the order had been received by the publisher, the company still balked at featuring the book on their website. Perhaps they viewed us as a poor customer or a difficult customer. In any event, they finally did put the book up on their site, sometime in May of 2004, the same month that the book was published. In the meantime, Dr. Rodeheaver lost an opportunity promote the book at two sociological meetings that he attended in the spring of 2004.

That spring, I received a promotional flyer from the publisher with a testimonial from an author whose prose was dripping with praise for the staff: how they had worked carefully with him on the content and design of the book and its cover; and how aggressively they had marketed the book. I felt that this was clearly false advertising, based on my experience. I received no such assistance. Maybe if the author is in a position to simply write a check for the cost of the 100 books, or is from a higher ranked school, the customer service is better. Frustrated at this point, it was difficult to imagine that my biggest disappointment with this particular publisher was still to come.

When the book arrived in May, 2004, the title of the book was misspelled on the cover page and on the spine. We contacted the publisher seven times over several months trying to correct this embarrassing error, only to be ignored or to be told that the publisher was looking into the problem. Angered, I filed a complaint with the Better Business Bureau in March, 2005. The publisher simply ignored the complaint, but they did tell Dan Rodeheaver that all the problems with the book had been taken care of. In reality, nothing had been done. We considered legal action at that point. Finally, in the fall of 2005, corrected copies of the book arrived at my office.

About the only thing that keeps me from being overly frustrated about my research program is to accentuate the positive and to look at the big picture and what is being expected of me by my university. By doing this, I can see that I am fulfilling the obligations of a tenure track position and that just about all my publications count, regardless of the problems that occur along the way. To better appreciate my situation, I often examine the vitae of sociology teachers in the upper tiers; their research records are much better and stronger than mine; and I can feel better about the security and the scaled-down publication requirement that Tier 4 affords. Making a list of the positives may help you, if in similar circumstances.

Service

The service requirement, once the recruit is aware of it, can be both a blessing and a curse. If the tenure candidate is not a strong researcher, the committee assignments can become a "way out" of the writing requirements; the committee work might substitute for the writing, if the supervisor is willing. On the other hand, if the recruit is good at research, the service requirement can be an extra burden, and a drain upon the young scholar's time and energy.

The service requirement usually encompasses service to the community and to the university. The community service requirement could be things such as presentations to service clubs, church groups, and schools; participation in local service organizations' events; and volunteering at the community, state or national level on an ongoing basis. Occasionally sociologists may be appointed to state or regional task forces by public officials. Any media activity related to the community requirement might also be considered for credit, if the supervisor is willing to count it.

The university requirement can include such items as serving on university committees, a requirement that can be a joy or headache depending upon how involved the assignment is. If the tenure candidate hates committee work, this can be a nightmare. Some committees may require an hour or more per week, and the responsibilities of the chair may be even more burdensome. Other assignments are less stressful, requiring less time or intensive effort only at certain times of the year. Evidence of student advising or mentoring is also usually a requirement for tenure, and this can be intermittently heavy during registration and pre-registration periods.

Special projects assigned to the professor or taken on by them may also part of the university service requirement; these may be self studies that are part of the accreditation process at your school, or can be special studies that require a considerable "front-end" effort before implementation, for example, the development of new degree programs or the conception and development of new and innovative presentation methods such as tele-courses, video-learning or distance learning classes.

The remainder of the requirement could be a potpourri of assignments that could be interesting or not, depending upon the personal interests of the professor: teaching overload or independent study courses; teaching writing enriched courses; sponsoring a student organization; making presentations to University organizations on campus; grant writing and the accompanying research; and volunteer work at a variety of campus events. It usually does not take long for the recruit to discover the activities that are the least appealing; in time these are jettisoned, left behind for newer faculty with less seniority.

Conclusion

The big picture presented here is the picture that might not be imagined early on by the new recruit to the teaching institutions. It is a picture of manifold joys and pains. At its best, the big picture involves an examination of a secure life and the knowledge that much good is being done. On balance, it is a life that appears to be preferred by many. One publication suggested that the modal sociologist today is a male in his fifties, living in the south.[48] Certainly, there are many at the bottom of sociology that could hold jobs in the upper tiers, and these people are aware that such a job could be much more difficult and stressful at that level. Knowing that, the mass of sociology looks better to them than the elite. As one Tier 4 faculty confided to the author: "I'm impressed with this faculty, they are serious about their jobs … (these are) hard working and productive people. A lot of good is being done here."[49]

3 A TEACHING EXAMPLE: THE STANFORD PRISON EXPERIMENT

One of classic experiments in sociology is remembered as a fiasco with disastrous results. In the late summer of 1971, the Stanford Prison Experiment had to be halted because of the bizarre behavior of the research subjects. In a mock prison established at Stanford University, the designated student "guards" had become sadistic, abusive, unreasonable, even subhuman. The designated student "prisoners," meanwhile, had begun to act as real prisoners, even forfeiting their right to simply quit or resign from the experiment, and asking instead for friends, family or lawyers to intervene on their behalf. Due to the depression and the psychological stress of the experiment on the prisoners, the planned two-week experiment had to be aborted after six days. Though the experiment occurred long ago, I thought that it would be an interesting topic for today's students to explore. This chapter is the story of the experiment itself, the lessons learned from it, and what several cohorts of introductory sociology students at a teaching institution of the millennial era got out of their exploration of the experiment.

Background of the Experiment

Technically, the experiment was a psychological experiment, as it was conducted by the Psychology Department at Stanford University under the direction of Phillip Zimbardo. However, the experiment was important to the closely related fields of criminology and sociology, and became a classic in both fields despite the negative outcome.

Research experimentation in psychology had showed promise and yielded important research results. However, attempts to expand the research to larger social groups proved troublesome. For example, social psychologist Muzafer Sherif conducted a field experiment with 12 year old boys at a summer camp, and the final stages of the experiment had to be curtailed because the boys were in danger of being seriously hurt.[50] The boys in the study were divided into two groups. Then, through the manipulations of the researchers, the groups were brought into competition and conflict. For a number of days the conflict was limited to apple-throwing fights and to raids on each other's cabins. But in a final severe confrontation in the dining hall, the two groups of boys faced off and the situation became dangerous. Some of the boys started to throw silverware and plates. The researchers quickly stepped in and stopped the hostilities, and also concluded that phase of the experiment.[51] The Stanley Milgram experiment was also controversial in that some of the subjects were lead to believe that they had administered potentially lethal electronic shocks to selected subjects in the study. Critics wondered about the psychological pain inflicted upon these subjects, who were harboring thoughts that they had just killed someone during a psychological experiment.[52] Ethical discussions ensued about how to better inform research subjects about the nature of their participation in experiments.

The research questions asked at the beginning of the Stanford experiment appeared to be more philosophical than experimental. What happens when you put good people in an evil place? Does humanity win over evil, or does evil triumph?[53] Absent in the experiment was the kind of experimental rigor one might expect from a study conducted at a Tier 1 school: the hypotheses were not clearly stated, there appeared to be no independent or dependent variable, and there was no control group. The "experiment" was basically exploratory research on the psychology of prison life.[54] Despite that, Professor Zimbardo proceeded with his unusual study in August of 1971. Much of the information summarized below is presented at the prison experiment's web page, and is presented here as contextual background information about the experiment.

The first step in participating in the study was for interested individuals to answer an ad in a local newspaper calling for people to volunteer in a study of the psychological effects of prison life. The research design called for setting up a simulated prison and then carefully noting the effects of this institution on the behavior of all those within its walls, including prisoners, guards, administration, and support staff.[55]

Diagnostic interviews and personality tests were given to more than 70 applicants who had answered the ad. This process eliminated candidates that might not fare well in the mock prison setting, such as those with psychological problems, medical disabilities, or a history of crime or drug abuse. After this screening, a sample of 24 college students remained. They were from the U.S. and Canada, they happened to be in the Stanford area, and wanted to earn $15 per day by participating in the study. On all dimensions that could be tested or observed by the research staff, they reacted normally.[56]

By flip of a coin, the healthy, intelligent, middle-class males were divided into two groups, one being randomly assigned to be the prison guards while the other group became prisoners. At the beginning, the researchers could see no difference at all between the young men in the two groups.[57]

In an effort to make the experiment as real as possible, the Stanford psychologists called upon the knowledge and experience of special consultants, including a former prisoner who had served nearly seventeen years behind bars. This person in turn was able to introduce the staff to a number of other ex-convicts and correctional personnel.[58]

The mock prison was constructed by boarding up each end of a corridor in the basement of Stanford's Psychology Department building. That corridor was "the yard" and was the only outside place where prisoners were allowed to walk, eat, or exercise, except to use the bathroom down the hallway. To create prison cells, the researchers took the doors off some laboratory rooms and replaced them with specially made doors with steel bars and cell numbers.[59]

Through a small opening at one end of the hall, researchers could videotape and record the events that occurred. On the side of the corridor opposite the cells was a small closet which became

"The Hole," or solitary confinement. It was dark and very confining, about two feet wide and two feet deep, but tall enough that a "bad prisoner" could stand up. Additionally, an intercom system allowed the researchers to secretly bug the cells to monitor what the prisoners discussed, and also to make public statements or announcements to the prisoners. There were no windows or clocks to judge the passage of time, which later resulted in some time-distorting experiences.[60] With these features in place, the Stanford "jail" was ready to receive its first prisoners.

The Experiment Begins

This very realistic experiment got under way on a Sunday morning in August, when a Palo Alto police car swept through the town picking up the soon to be student prisoners for violations of the Armed Robbery and Burglary penal codes. Each suspect was picked up at his home, charged, warned of his legal rights, spread-eagled against the police car, searched, and handcuffed – often as surprised and curious neighbors looked on. The suspect was then put in the rear of the police car and carried off to the police station, sirens wailing. The car arrived at the station, the suspect was brought inside, formally booked, again warned of his Miranda rights, finger printed, and a complete identification was made. The suspect was then taken to a holding cell where he was left blindfolded to ponder his fate and to wonder what he had done to get himself into this mess. Later, the prisoners were put into a car and driven to the "Stanford County Jail" for further processing.The prisoners were brought into the experimental prison one at a time and greeted by the warden, who conveyed the seriousness of their offense and their new status as prisoners.[61]

Next, the prisoners went through a "degradation procedure" whose purpose was in part to humiliate prisoners and to strip them of their identity, and in part to be sure they weren't bringing in any germs to contaminate the jail. This procedure was similar to the real life experiences of ex-inmates in the state of Texas' prison system. Each prisoner was systematically searched and stripped naked. He was then deloused with a spray, to convey the belief of the research staff that he may have germs or lice.[62]

Prisoners then received a uniform; the main part of this uniform was a dress, or smock, which each prisoner wore at all times with no underclothes. On the smock, in front and in back, was his prison ID number. On each prisoner's right ankle was a heavy chain, bolted on and worn at all times. Rubber sandals were the foot-ware, and each prisoner covered his hair with a stocking cap made from a woman's nylon stocking.[63]

It's important to note that the psychologists were trying to create a functional simulation of a prison and not a literal prison. As noted on the Stanford Prison Experiment web site, real male prisoners don't wear dresses, but real male prisoners do feel humiliated and do feel emasculated. The goal was to produce similar effects quickly by putting men in a dress without any underclothes. As soon as some of the prisoners were put in these uniforms they began to walk and to sit differently, and to hold themselves differently, more like a woman than like a man.[64]

It is also uncommon in most prisons for the prisoners to have chains on their feet. Here, the chains were used to remind prisoners of the oppressiveness of their environment. Even when prisoners were asleep, they could not escape the atmosphere of oppression. When a prisoner turned over, the chain would hit his other foot, waking him up and reminding him that he was still in prison, unable to escape even by dreaming about being somewhere else.[65]

Prisoners were made to feel anonymous by use of ID numbers. Each prisoner had to be called only by his ID number and could only refer to himself and the other prisoners by number.[66]

Instead of shaving each prisoner's head, they were issued stocking caps to wear. Again, the idea here is to approximate the conditions of a functional prison and not to create the actual conditions of a real prison. The process of having one's head shaved, which takes place in most prisons as well as in the military, is designed in part to minimize each person's individuality, since some people show their individuality through hair style or length. It is also a way of getting people to begin complying with the arbitrary, coercive rules of the institution.[67]

The guards received no formal kind of staff training on how to be guards. They had freedom within reasonable limits to do whatever they thought was necessary to maintain law and order in the prison, and to command the respect of the prisoners. The guards made up their own set of rules, which they then carried into effect under the supervision of an undergraduate from Stanford University. The situation was similar to that in the Abu Ghraib scandal, where national guardsmen found themselves supervising an Iraqi prison with little guidance or training. The student guards at Stanford were warned, however, of the potential seriousness of their mission and of the possible dangers in the situation they were about to enter. Obviously, real guards who voluntarily take such a dangerous job receive similar warnings, whether it be at Abu Ghraib or at any other correctional facility.[68]

The experimental prisoners expected some harassment, to have their privacy and some of their other civil rights violated while they were in prison, and to get a minimally adequate diet. This was not a surprise to them; it was part of the informed consent agreement they signed when they volunteered.[69]

All guards were dressed in identical uniforms of khaki, and they carried a whistle around their neck and a billy club borrowed from the police. Guards also wore special sun-glasses, mirrored ones that prevented anyone from seeing their eyes or reading their emotions, and thus helped to further promote their anonymity. The research design called for studying not only the prisoners but also the guards, who found themselves in a new power-laden role.[70]

The experiment began with nine guards and nine prisoners. Three guards worked each of the three eight-hour shifts, while three prisoners occupied each of the three barren cells around the clock. The remaining guards and prisoners from the sample of 24 students were on call in case they were needed. The cells were very small, so much so that there was room for only three cots on which the prisoners slept or sat, with little room for anything else.[71]

Early in the morning, at 2:30 A.M., the prisoners were awakened by blasting whistles for the first of many "counts." The counts served the purpose of familiarizing the prisoners with their numbers as counts took place several times each shift and often at night. More importantly, these staged events provided a regular occasion for the guards to exercise control over the prisoners. Initially at least, the prisoners were not completely into their roles and did not take the counts too seriously; they were still trying at this point in time to assert their independence. The guards were also getting acquainted with their new roles and were not yet sure how to assert authority or control over their prisoners. This turned out to be the start of several direct confrontations between the guards and prisoners.[72]

To punish infractions of the rules or displays of improper attitudes toward the guards or institution, push-ups became a common form of punishment. When the guards demanded push-ups from the prisoners, the researchers at first thought this was an inappropriate kind of punishment for a prison (real or simulated), a rather juvenile and minimal form of punishment, similar to frat-house hazing. But, the staff was surprised to learn later that push-ups were often used as a form of punishment in Nazi concentration camps, as discovered in the drawing of a former concentration camp inmate. One of the student guards also stepped on the prisoners' backs while they did push-ups, or made other prisoners sit or step on the backs of fellow prisoners doing their push-ups.[73]

Rebellion

As there were no incidents on the first day, the staff was caught off guard by the rebellion that swept the prison on the morning of the second day. The prisoners removed their stocking caps, ripped off their numbers, and barricaded themselves inside the cells by putting their beds against the door. What would the guards do about this situation? They were quite angry and frustrated because the prisoners also began to taunt and curse them. When the morning shift of guards came on, they became upset at the night shift who, they felt, must have been too lenient.[74] The guards had to handle the rebellion themselves, and the staff was intrigued by what happened next.

To begin, the guards insisted that reinforcements be called in. The three guards who were waiting on stand-by call at home came in, and the night shift of guards voluntarily remained on duty to bolster the morning shift. The guards met and decided to treat force with force. They got a fire extinguisher which shot a stream of cold carbon dioxide, and they forced the prisoners away from the doors.[75]

Each cell was broken into by the guards, each prisoner stripped naked, the beds were taken out, and the ringleaders of the prisoner rebellion were put into solitary confinement. The guards generally began to harass and intimidate the prisoners.[76]

The rebellion was snuffed, but a new problem arose quickly to take its place. Nine guards with clubs could subdue the nine prisoners, but the study had been structured in such a way that nine guards could not be on duty all at the same time – there would be no way for any break time or any time off, for that matter. Moreover, the budget of the experiment did not allow for hiring more guards, or even for having them all work together at once. One of the guards came up a solution. "Let's use psychological tactics instead of physical ones."[77] Psychological tactics amounted to setting up a privilege cell.

The staff decided to designate one of the three cells as a "privilege cell." The three prisoners least involved in the rebellion were given special privileges. They got their uniforms back, got their beds back, and were allowed to wash and brush their teeth. The others were not. Privileged prisoners also got to eat special food in the presence of the other prisoners who had temporarily lost the privilege of eating.[78] This continued for about half a day before tactics were changed.

To confuse the prisoners as much as they could, the guards then took some of these "good" prisoners and put them into the "bad" cells, and took some of the "bad" prisoners and put them into the "good" cell. Some of the prisoners who were the ringleaders now thought that the prisoners from the privileged cell must be informers, and suddenly, the prisoners became distrustful of each other. The ex-convict consultants later informed the staff that a similar tactic is used by real guards in real prisons to break prisoner alliances.[79]

Another unexpected outcome of the rebellion was the producing of greater solidarity among the guards. The guards no longer perceived the prison as an experiment or a simple simulation. Now, the guards saw the prisoners as troublemakers who were out to get them, who might really cause them some harm. In response to this threat, the guards began stepping up their control, surveillance, and aggression.[80]

At this point in the experiment, virtually all aspects of prisoners' behavior fell under the total and arbitrary control of the guards. Even going to the toilet became a privilege which a guard could grant or deny at his whim. After each night's 10:00 P.M. lights out "lock-up," prisoners were often forced to urinate or defecate in a bucket that was left in their cell. On occasion the guards would not allow prisoners to empty these buckets. Soon the prison began to smell of urine and feces -- further adding to the degrading quality of the environment.[81]

The ringleader of the rebellion was singled out for especially harsh treatment. He was a heavy smoker, and they controlled him by regulating his opportunity to smoke. Later the staff learned, while censoring the prisoners' mail, that he was a self-styled radical activist. He had volunteered in order to "expose" the experiment, which he mistakenly thought was an establishment tool to find ways to control student radicals. In fact, he had planned to sell the story to an underground newspaper when the experiment was over. However, even he fell so completely into the role of prisoner that he was proud to be elected leader of the Stanford County Jail Grievance Committee, as revealed in a letter to his girlfriend.[82]

Less than three days into the experiment, one of the prisoners was reportedly suffering from acute emotional disturbance, disorganized thinking, crying, and rage. In spite of all of this, the staff had already come to think so much like prison authorities that they thought the prisoner was trying to "con" them in an attempt to gain his release. When a prison consultant interviewed this particular prisoner, the consultant chided him for being so weak, and told him what kind of abuse he could expect from the guards and the prisoners if he were in San Quentin Prison. The prisoner was then given the offer of becoming an informant in exchange for no further guard harassment.[83]

This prisoner told other prisoners at the next count, "You can't leave. You can't quit." That sent a chilling message and heightened their sense of really being imprisoned. The prisoner then began to act "crazy," to scream, to curse, to go into a rage that seemed out of control. It took quite a while before the staff became convinced that he was really suffering and that he needed to be released.[84]

Public Scrutiny

The following day, the staff held a visiting hour for parents and friends. Dr. Zimbardo and associates were worried that when the parents saw the state of the mock jail, they might insist on taking their sons home. To counter this, Zimbardo manipulated both the situation and the visitors by making the prison environment seem pleasant and benign. As he notes on the web site, the prisoners were washed, shaved, and groomed; they cleaned and polished their cells; and, they were fed a big dinner. Music was played on the intercom, and a former Stanford cheerleader was recruited to greet the visitors at the registration desk.[85]

As the visitors arrived, the staff manipulated their behavior and brought it under the staff's situational control. Visitors had to register, were made to wait half an hour, were told that only two visitors could see any one prisoner, were limited to only ten minutes of visiting time, and had to be under the surveillance of a guard during the visit. Before any parents could enter the visiting area, they also had to discuss their son's case with the Warden. Parents complained about these arbitrary rules, but remarkably, they complied with them.[86]

Observing how fatigued and stressed their sons looked, a few parents got upset with the staff. Amazingly, their reaction was to work within the system to appeal privately to the Superintendent to make conditions better for their boy. When one mother told me she had never seen her son looking so bad, Zimbardo responded by shifting the blame from the situation to her son. "What's the matter with your boy? Doesn't he sleep
well?" Then he asked the father, "Don't you think your boy can handle this?" The father replied, "Of course he can -- he's a real tough kid, a leader."[87]

The Escape Plot

In the drama unfolding at the mock prison, the next major event that the staff had to contend with was a rumored mass escape plot. One of the guards overheard the prisoners talking about an escape that would take place immediately after visiting hours. The rumor that circulated went like this: the prisoner showing the signs of extreme stress that had been released the night before, was going to round up a bunch of his friends and break in to free the prisoners.[88]

At this point, the staff showed evidence of having adopted the "prison staff mode" and were not really thinking nor acting like experimental social psychologists. Instead of recording the pattern of rumor transmission and preparing to observe the impending escape, the staff reacted with concern about the security of the prison. The staff held a strategy session with the Warden, the Superintendent, and one of the chief lieutenants, to plan how to foil the escape.[89]

Afterwards, the staff decided to put an informant (an experimental confederate) in the cell that #8612 (the stressed prisoner that was released) had occupied. The job of the informant would be to give information about the escape plot. Meanwhile, Dr. Zimbardo asked the Palo Alto Police Department if inmates could be transferred from the mock jail to one of the city's old jails. The request was turned down because the Palo Alto Police would not be covered by their insurance carrier if prisoners were moved into their jail. Zimbardo, now totally into the role of prison administrator, left angry and disgusted at this lack of cooperation from the city.[90]

Then the staff formulated a second plan. The plan was to dismantle the mock jail after the visitors left, call in more guards, chain the prisoners together, put bags over their heads, and transport them to a fifth floor storage room until after the anticipated break in. When the conspirators came, Dr. Zimbardo would be sitting there alone. He would tell them that the experiment was over and he had sent all of their friends home, that there was nothing left to liberate. After they left, the prisoners come back and security is redoubled at the prison. Zimbardo's notes say that he even thought of luring #8612 back on some pretext and then imprisoning him again because he was released on false pretenses.[91]

The prison break turned out to be just a rumor. It never materialized. The reaction showed just how deeply internalized their mock prison roles had become. The staff had spent an entire day planning to foil the escape, begging the police department for help, moving the prisoners to another location, and dismantling most of the prison. They were so busy that they collected no data at all. An opportunity to study the social psychological processes in rumor development was tragically lost, but instead the staff was more frustrated about the fact that they had lost control of the prisoners, had allowed the prisoners to fool them, and had been unable to even the score in this situation. As Dr. Zimbardo writes on the web site, the staff was very angry, and someone was going to pay for this.[92]

The prisoners ended up paying the price. The guards again escalated very noticeably their level of harassment, increasing the humiliation they made the prisoners suffer, forcing them to do menial, repetitive work such as cleaning out toilet bowls with their bare hands. The guards had prisoners do push-ups, jumping jacks, whatever the guards could think up, and they increased the length of the counts to several hours each.[93]

Nearing The End

At this point in the study, Zimbardo invited a Catholic priest who had been a prison chaplain to evaluate how realistic the prison situation was, and the result was truly astonishing or "Kafkaesque" as the principal investigator wrote in his notes. The chaplain interviewed each prisoner individually, and Dr. Zimbardo watched in amazement as half the prisoners introduced themselves by number rather than name. After some small talk, he popped the key question: "Son, what are you doing to get out of here?"[94] When the prisoners responded with puzzlement, he explained that the only way to get out of prison was with the help of a lawyer. He then volunteered to contact their parents to get legal aid if they wanted him to, and some of the prisoners accepted his offer. There was no discussion of negotiating a release or of simply resigning the study; hopes of that had faded long ago.[95]

Only one prisoner did not want to speak to the priest - prisoner #819, who was feeling sick, had refused to eat, and wanted to see a doctor. Eventually he was persuaded to come out of his cell and talk to the priest and superintendent so Zimbardo could see for himself what kind of a doctor he needed. While talking to the staff, he broke down and began to cry hysterically, just as had the other two boys released earlier. Dr. Zimbardo took the chain off his foot, the cap off his head, and told him to go and rest in a room that was adjacent to the prison yard. Zimbardo promised that he would get the prisoner some food and then take him to see a doctor. In the meantime, he heard fellow prisoners mocking him and shouting insults. Zimbardo returned quickly to the room where he had left the prisoner, and found the boy sobbing uncontrollably while in the background his fellow prisoners were yelling that he was a bad prisoner. No longer was the chanting disorganized and full of fun, as it had been on the first day. Now it was marked by strict conformity and compliance, as if a single voice was saying, "#819 is bad."[96]

Dr. Zimbardo suggested that the prisoner exit the study now, but the prisoner refused. He said that he could not leave because the others had labeled him a bad prisoner. Even though he was feeling sick, he wanted to go back and prove to his peers that he was not a bad prisoner.[97]

At that point Zimbardo said, "Listen, you are not #819. You are [his name], and my name is Dr. Zimbardo. I am a psychologist, not a prison superintendent, and this is not a real prison. This is just an experiment, and those are students, not prisoners, just like you. Let's go."[98] Zimbardo's notes said: "He stopped crying suddenly, looked up at me like a small child awakened from a nightmare, and replied, 'Okay, let's go.'"[99]

The following day, all prisoners who thought they had grounds for being paroled were chained together and individually brought before the Parole Board. The Board was composed mainly of people who were strangers to the prisoners (departmental secretaries and graduate students) and was headed by one of the prison consultants.[100]

The parole hearings produced anomalous results. First, when the prisoners were asked whether they would forfeit the money they had earned up to that time if we were to parole them, most said that "yes," they would. Then, when the hearing was over and prisoners were ordered back to their cells while the staff considered their requests, every prisoner obeyed, even though they could have achieved the same result by simply quitting the experiment. Why did they obey? Zimbardo believed that it was because they powerless to resist. The prisoners' sense of reality had shifted, and they no longer perceived their imprisonment as an experiment. In the psychological prison that had been created, only the correctional staff had the power to grant paroles.[101]

At the parole hearings the staff also witnessed an unexpected transformation of the prison consultant as he adopted the role of head of the Parole Board. He literally became the most hated authoritarian official imaginable, so much so that when it was over he felt sick at who he had become. He had managed to personify his own tormentor who had previously rejected his annual parole requests for 16 years when he was a prisoner.[102]

By day five, the staff could identify three types of guards. First, there were tough but fair guards who followed prison rules. Second, there were "good guys" who did little favors for the prisoners and never punished them. And then, about a third of the guards were hostile, arbitrary, and inventive in their forms of prisoner humiliation. These guards appeared to thoroughly enjoy the power they wielded, yet none of the preliminary personality tests were able to predict this behavior. The only link between personality and prison behavior was a finding that prisoners with a high degree of authoritarianism endured our authoritarian prison environment longer than did other prisoners.[103] This kind of guard appeared to most resemble the abusive guards observed in photographs at the Abu Ghraib prison in 2003.

The prisoners nicknamed the most macho and brutal guard in the study "John Wayne." Later, Zimbardo's staff learned that the most notorious guard in a Nazi prison near Buchenwald was named "Tom Mix", or the John Wayne of an earlier generation, because of his "Wild West" cowboy macho image in abusing camp inmates.[104]

Exactly how and where had the experiment's version of "John Wayne" learned to become such a guard? How could he and others move so readily into that role? How could intelligent, mentally healthy, "ordinary" men become perpetrators of evil so quickly? These were questions that the staff was forced to ask.[105]

Prisoners felt feelings of frustration and powerlessness, and expressed this in a variety of ways. At first, some prisoners rebelled or fought with the guards. Four prisoners reacted by breaking down emotionally as a way to escape the situation. One prisoner developed a psychosomatic rash over his entire body when he learned that his parole request had been turned down. Others tried to cope by being good prisoners, doing everything the guards wanted them to do. One of them was even nicknamed "Sarge," because he was so military-like in executing all commands.[106]

The End of the Experiment

Near the end, the prisoners were disintegrated, both as a group and as individuals. Group unity vanished; what was left was a bunch of isolated individuals hanging on, much like prisoners of war or hospitalized mental patients. The guards had won total control of the prison, and they commanded the blind obedience of each prisoner.

The mock prison had become a total institution, not far removed from what prisons are in real life.[107]

There was one final act of rebellion. Prisoner #416 was newly admitted as one of our stand-by prisoners. Unlike the other prisoners, who had experienced a gradual escalation of harassment, this prisoner's horror was full-blown when he arrived. The veteran prisoners told him that quitting was impossible, that it was a real prison.[108]

Prisoner #416 protested the experiment by going on a hunger strike to force his release. After several unsuccessful attempts to get #416 to eat, the guards threw him into solitary confinement for three hours, even though their own rules stated that one hour was the limit. Still, #416 refused.[109]

It was logical to assume at this point that #416 should have been a hero to the other prisoners. Instead, the others saw him as a "problem" and a troublemaker. The head guard then exploited this feeling by giving prisoners a choice. They could have #416 come out of solitary if they were willing to give up their blanket, or they could leave #416 in solitary all night.[110] Most elected to keep their blanket and let their fellow prisoner suffer in solitary all night.[111]

Some visiting parents asked Zimbardo to contact a lawyer in order to get their son out of prison on the fifth night. They said a Catholic priest had called to tell them they should get a lawyer or public defender if they wanted to bail their son out. Zimbardo called the lawyer as requested, and he came the next day to interview the prisoners with a standard set of legal questions, even though he, too, knew it was just an experiment.[112]

By now, it became clear to the staff that the end of the study was drawing near. They had created an overwhelmingly powerful situation, one where the prisoners were withdrawing and behaving in pathological ways, and in which some of the guards were behaving sadistically. Even the "good" guards felt helpless to do anything to rectify the situation, and none of the guards quit while the study was in progress. No guard ever came late for his shift, called in sick, left early, or demanded extra pay for overtime work.[113]

Dr. Zimbardo and his staff ended the study prematurely for two reasons. First, the group of researchers had learned through videotapes that the guards were escalating their abuse of prisoners in the middle of the night when they thought no researchers were watching and the experiment was "off." Their boredom had driven them to ever more pornographic and degrading abuse of the prisoners.[114]

Second, a recent Stanford Ph.D. brought in to conduct interviews with the guards and prisoners strongly objected when she saw prisoners being marched on a toilet run, bags over their heads, legs chained together, hands on each other's shoulders. Filled with outrage, she said, "It's terrible what you are doing to these boys!"[115] Out of 50 outsiders who had seen the prison, she was the only one who ever questioned its morality. The staff took her objection seriously, and after only six days, the planned two-week prison simulation was called off.[116]

Lessons Learned From The Experiment

The study was terminated on August 20, 1971. The next day, there was an alleged escape attempt at San Quentin State Prison in California. Prisoners in the Maximum Adjustment Center were released from their cells by George Jackson, who had smuggled a gun into the prison. Several guards and some informant prisoners were tortured and murdered during the attempt, but the escape was prevented after the leader was allegedly gunned down while trying to scale the 30-foot high prison walls.[117]

Soon afterward, less than one month later, prisons made more news when a riot erupted at Attica Prison in New York. After weeks of negotiations with prisoners who held guards hostage while demanding basic human rights, New York Governor Nelson Rockefeller ordered the National Guard to take back the prison by full force. A great many guards and prisoners were killed and injured by that ill-advised decision.[118]

An important demand of the prisoners at Attica was that they be treated like human beings. After observing the simulated prison for only six days, Zimbardo's staff could understand how prisons dehumanize people, turning them into objects and instilling in them feelings of hopelessness. As for the guards, they realized how ordinary people could be readily transformed from "the good Dr. Jekyll to the evil Mr. Hyde."[119]

As Zimbardo notes, in the decades since the experiment took place, prison conditions and correctional policies in the United States became even more punitive and destructive. He is convinced that the worsening of conditions has been a result of the politicization of corrections, with politicians vying for who is toughest on crime, along with the racialization of arrests and sentencing, with African-Americans and Hispanics overrepresented. The media has also contributed to the problem by generating “moral panics” that heightened fear of violent crimes even as statistics show that violent crimes have decreased.[120]

Zimbardo also notes that there are more Americans in prisons than ever before. According to a Justice Department survey, the number of jailed Americans more than doubled during the past 12 years, with over 1.8 million people in jail or prison by the late 1990s.[121]

The study also brought up a number of questions unique to such exploratory social research. Because the purpose was to study a very broad question, the psychology of prison life, it is very difficult to define specifically what the data are, or what the data are supposed to be. It seems that just about everything that was happening was “data” to be later studied from the videotapes. Then there is the issue of opportunities for study that were tragically lost, mostly because the staff had adopted the mode of real prison employees and had forgotten about the research. This leads to the further question of what could have been done to minimize the effects of experimenter bias on the outcome of the study. Having more outside monitors would have appeared to be the answer, but who is to say that they too would not have been caught up in the action? And what were the dangers of the principal investigator assuming the role of prison superintendent? You could also make the suggestion that this role should have been assumed by an off site researcher far removed from the day to day workings of the mock prison.[122]

In the summer of 2004, the Stanford Prison Experiment made the news again. In Iraq, a poorly supervised group of national guardsmen had taken charge of the supervision of Iraqi prisoners, some suspected to be terrorists. With a nod and a wink from military intelligence, the guardsmen appeared to have total control of the process of how intelligence information was gathered, with an apparent emphasis on the final result, and not so much how the result was obtained. People who remembered the Stanford experiment remembered how quickly the whole experiment had degenerated into chaos, and wondered if the same dynamic was at work in the Abu Ghraib prison. Did evil triumph over good once again, just as it had 23 years ago in Palo Alto? For many the answer was yes, and was a reminder of what can happen when supervision is minimal, and individuals are suddenly given power beyond their capacity to absorb.[123]

Millennial Students Meet the Stanford Experiment

Beginning in 2000, I began to search for an assignment for introductory sociology students, one that they would find memorable, and one from which they might take away some valuable lessons in life. I settled on the Stanford Prison Experiment because the age of the students involved in the study was about the same as the average age of the students in my introductory class; and, the experiment did deal with some of the issues that students face in daily life on campus - the triumph of evil over good, peer pressure, the development of personal identity and roles, and rapid social change that leaves confusion in its wake. I thought that by putting each student in the shoes of the students in the Stanford Prison Experiment, those millennial students might learn something about themselves as they contemplate how they might have reacted to the experiment, if time and unforeseen circumstances had managed to put them in such a situation. Among other things, the experiment probably made them very pessimistic about taking part in any ongoing psychology experiments that were underway on their campus.

Beginning in 2001, I suspended my introductory sociology classes for a day, and asked the students to spend time outside of class to work on an "Internet assignment" about the Stanford Prison Experiment. I asked them to visit the Experiment's web site at www.prisonexp.org and to read the introductory page. After that, they were invited to go through the slide show in its entirety. That show essentially tells the story of the experiment that I've summarized above, and includes still photos and video clips from the experiment, adding to the realism for the student. After the student has gone through the slide show in its entirety, I asked them to answer several questions about the experiment, most of them suggested by Phillip Zimbardo as discussion questions that help people to reflect upon the experiment:

1. What police procedures are used during arrests, and how do these procedures lead people to feel confused, fearful, and dehumanized?

2. If you were a guard, what type of guard would you have become? How sure are you?

3. What prevented "good guards" from objecting or countermanding the orders from tough or bad guards?

4. If you were a prisoner, would you have been able to endure the experience? What would you have done differently than those subjects did? If you were imprisoned in a "real" prison for five years or more, could you take it?

5. Why did our prisoners try to work within the arbitrary prison system to effect a change in it (e.g., setting up a Grievance Committee), rather than trying to dismantle or change the system through outside help?

6. What was the most important thing that you learned from the Stanford Prison Experiment?

The answers to the questions could be handwritten or typed, and were to be handed in to the instructor to be graded before the end of the semester. As most of the questions were subjective, I graded the assignments based upon how thoroughly the student answered the question and how much detail they used from the historical facts of the study in answering the questions.

Question 1 was probably the most "objective," in the sense that Dr. Zimbardo had arranged the experiment so that the students' experience of being arrested would be realistic. Thus, all the student had to do to answer this particular question was to relate how the student prisoners in the experiment were treated by the arresting officers. This material was directly from the slide show. However, some students interpreted the question to mean *today's* police procedures in general that dehumanize the arrestee, and thus answered the question with recent experiences that they had heard or read about in their community.

Questions 2-4 were very subjective, and are self-reflection kinds of questions. I could not possibly anticipate anyone's answer, and instructed students to be honest. I did so at the risk that such an assignment only reinforces the widespread view among students that sociology is nothing more than one's opinion about social reality. Nonetheless, I continue to ask the questions each semester, because they provide a window into the student's personality and you get some feeling that you've come to know the student personally – something that may be difficult to do in more conventional ways at the medium to large sized teaching institutions. I usually held on to the assignments for years, just in case a student approached me later for advice or for a letter of recommendation. Especially if I did not know the student very well, the answers to the questions provided some contextual information that might be useful in evaluating the student.

Question 5 is more objective than questions 2-4, but at the same time, allows for some individuality to come forth in the responses. Among other things, the response to this question might be an indicator of how closely the student was paying attention to the information about the experiment. On this question an answer that I expected to see was this: the prisoners, like everyone else in the experiment, had internalized the role assigned to them, and no longer felt that they could simply resign from the experiment. The experiment had come to be the social reality for the prisoners. However, I received other kinds of answers to this question and accepted them.

Question 6 is the one I most enjoy reading; and as long as students continue to say that they learned something from the experiment, I will probably continue to assign it. Just about everyone was able to cite something specific that they took away from the exercise.

The answers to the questions were fairly predictable for question 1 as it could be taken right from some of the slides in the slide show. Most students got the point that the arrest was supposed to be realistic and humiliating, and to clearly show who was in charge and who was going to be punished. Interestingly, many students generalized their answers to the question so as to include the tactics employed by all the authority figures in the experiment and not just the arresting officers. As one student put it:

> They arrested them in front of neighbors and

> family, stripped them, made them wear a "mock dress," put a bag over their head, and "debugged" them by spraying them down. They were not able to use the restroom in private.[124]

Additionally, as mentioned earlier, some interpreted the question to mean the tactics of today's police and answered accordingly, with arrests that they had read about or seen on TV, or perhaps even with something they'd seen in their neighborhood.

What type of guard would you have been, and how sure are you of this? This was the second question, and is an interesting question from my standpoint because it helps me to get to know something of the student's personality and their honest assessment (hopefully) of how they might have reacted to the situation, if thrust into it. Table 7

Table 7. Stanford Prison Experiment Question Two, Part A: What Type of Guard Would You Have Been?

Tough & Fair	Good Guy or Good Girl	Tough, Hostile	Don't Know/ Not Sure	Didn't answer question/ misunderstood question/ cannot classify answer
202 (31.5%)	229 (35.7%)	121 (18.9%)	24 (3.7%)	65 (10.1%)

shows the students' answers to the question. The largest group of students professed to be the "good guys" or "good girls" types of guards. Many stated that they were nice people, that being nice was part of their personality, and that they did not enjoy seeing others suffer:

> I would be a good guy guard. I would be like

> them because they do little favors for the prisoners and never punished them. The reason I picked them is because I'm a very nice person and I wouldn't treat someone so harsh like they (bad guards) treat the prisoners.[125]
>
> I am very sure that I would have been a good guard because I am a very lenient person. I don't like to hurt people purposely.[126]

A substantial group said they would have been "tough but fair," noting that they were raised in such a manner; and many said that they had children of their own now and this was how they wanted to raise their own kids. A surprising number (18.9%) admitted that they would have become hostile just like the "bad guard" students in the experiment. These students admitted that to do otherwise would have led to a loss of respect among the prisoners and to a loss of control. I teach in Louisiana, a conservative "Red" state that is heavily Republican and a "law and order' kind of place. Some of these students who said they would have been tough or hostile said they come from military or law enforcement families, and therefore had little sympathy for anyone in a prisoner role, even in a mock prison.

The second part, or part B of question two had to do with how sure the person was that they would be the type of guard that they had mentioned in the first part. Well over fifty percent said that they were pretty sure of the type of guard they would be, and I often wonder whether these young charges of mine really grasped the basic conclusion from the study, that even "normal" people can behave badly when put in the wrong social environment. I was more reassured by the substantial minority that, after saying what kind of guard they would have become, qualified their answer by saying that they could not be sure; after all, the participants in the Stanford study could not have predicted the bizarre outcome. Farrell Levy, for example, wrote:

> If I were a guard I would be a good guard, or at least I hope I would. Even the best people, when put under the wrong circumstances, can

> turn into that which they seek to fight against. So while I would start out as a good guard and strive to maintain my stand, unforeseen events might try to alter my position.[127]

Others similarly qualified their initial statements:

> I would hope I would be a good guard, but it is hard to say because I am rarely given that sort of power.[128]
>
> I have a feeling that I would have started out being a "good" guard and then later I would have become a "bad" guard. I think this only because when I am in charge I like the people I am in charge of to listen to me and I would not have reacted very well to the prisoners' harassment and cursing.[129]

In question 3, regarding what prevented the good guards from objecting to the orders of the bad guards, most students got the point that peer pressure or fear was involved; the good guy types were just not strong enough or did not have the kinds of personalities to override the more authoritarian type bad guards.

Question 4 asked if the student were in the place of the Stanford prisoners, could they have taken the experiment. Most said no, and said that they would have somehow been able to distinguish the experiment from the reality. They would have simply resigned, remembering that they were just participating in an experiment. Almost universally, the students said they would not be able to withstand a long stay in a real prison.

In question 5, the students were asked why the student prisoners worked within the arbitrary system that had been set up, and did not try to change the system. Most indicated that the situation had become real for the prisoners, and that they were acting like real prisoners.

In question 6, the introductory students were asked to relate what they learned from the experiment. Answers varied, as it was expected that each person may take away something different from the experience of watching the slide show and reflecting upon it. A few examples:

> If you are ever put in any kind of prison, it's important that you hold onto whatever morality or sanity you have, because you are not going to gain any in prison.[130]
>
> People change according to their environments. One never knows how he/she will really react until he/she goes through it.[131]
>
> People can change into another role quicker than I thought, and they really started acting like real prisoners quickly without knowing they were changing.[132]

Afterword

The assignment about the Stanford experiment appeared to resonate with today's students; I feel that if nothing else, it gets them away from a traditional lecture and an opportunity to spend time on a more technological kind of project, which many enjoy anyway. More important, though, is that the assignment appears to be memorable and something that they may retain from the class well after it is over. The Abu Ghraib scandal of 2004 appeared to illustrate the timeless nature of the experiment; I feel confidant that whenever events like that scandal occur in the future, the Stanford Prison Experiment will be mentioned again.

4 A RESEARCH EXAMPLE: MILITIA GROUPS OF THE 1990S

As data-gatherers, sociologists were initially inattentive to the rise of the U.S citizen militia movement in the 1990s. Except for Sean O'Brien and Donald Haider-Markel's examination of social correlates of rates of militia activity and James Aho's work on Idaho Christian Patriots, sociological investigations yielding quantitative or qualitative data were limited at best.[133] True, researchers have studied the Right wing and revolutionary right from a social movement perspective,[134] or under the rubric of domestic terrorism,[135] and some of the subjects studied were possibly militiamen or women, given that memberships in extreme right groups often overlap.[136] However, qualitative or quantitative data are lacking in these studies. Some, such as Betty Dobratz and Stephanie Shanks-Meile, clearly state that their work is not specifically about persons in militias.[137]

The overall lack of sociological interest is unexpected, given that sociologists have long been interested in the role that "anomie" or feelings of powerlessness play in peasant rebellions, protest movements, and related phenomena. Robert Merton for instance, contended that rebels, feeling the strain of living up to cultural goals and the established means of achieving them, reject and substitute both the culturally prescribed goals as well as the institutionalized means of achieving those goals.[138] Neil Smelser similarly approached revolutions and radical social movements from the standpoint of strain. He wrote that people join radical movements because they experience social dislocation in the form of social strain, especially when such strain springs from rapid social change. These social movements reassure participants that something is being done to redress the underlying source of strain.[139] Smelser asserted that several specific conditions follow the appearance of strain and that, altogether, the five conditions he identified are necessary and sufficient conditions for radical social movements such as militias to occur.[140] Militias qualify as radical movements because of their strong anti government rhetoric and general support for extreme measures to prevent America's slide into collectivism. Militia presence and activity on the Internet, then, is a phenomenon that can be studied within the framework of Smelser's theory. Militia watchers contend that those who join militias have experienced the kinds of social strains and other conditions to which Smelser refers.[141] Further, scholars argue that the Internet has become a forum for expressing such strains.[142]

The purpose of this chapter is to analyze the content of Internet traffic of U.S. militias in order to test Smelser's general thesis. We use militia Web sites and militia messages posted to Usenet as primary data to test his theory and to help fill a research gap in our knowledge of citizen militias. This study is among the first sociological studies of militias with an Internet presence, and one of the first in which militias from all regions of the U.S. are studied, and primary data collected. Additionally, it is among the first sociological studies that provide a conceptual and operational definition of a citizen militia.

Review of the Literature

The roots of today's militia movement lie in the revolutionary role of the militia in U.S. colonial history and the precedents for militias that appear in the Articles of Confederation, the U.S. Constitution, and subsequent federal legislation. This early U.S. experience solidified a republican tradition of an unorganized, armed populace whose function is to safeguard against the tyranny of standing armies and government incumbents.[143]

Early militias of the modern era (1958-1991) drew upon this tradition. Militia members of this era viewed their basic role as protectors of America against a global collectivist takeover.[144]

Beyond this similarity, however, early modern militias diverged philosophically along two different lines of thought. Each line brought a definition to the collective force trying to dominate the United States.

"Constitutionalists" believed in the sanctity of the U.S. Constitution and contended that certain groups were conspiring to destroy America. They were reluctant to blame a definite ethnic, racial, or religious group.[145] Important in the early stages of constitutionalism was the encouragement and support it drew from tax protesters, the Posse Comitatus, the John Birch Society, and the Mormon church.[146]

Originating from the second line of thought, Christian Identity ideology is built around three premises. First, white Aryans are descendants of the biblical tribes of Israel and are on earth to do God's work. Second, Jews are unconnected to the Israelites and are actually children of the devil. Third, the world is on the verge of a final apocalyptic struggle between good and evil, or between the Aryans and the global Jewish conspiracy.[147] Here, the "evil" collectivist force is international Jewry and its allies. The American version of Christian Identity developed through C. A. L. Totten, Howard Rand, and William Cameron. Following a period of consolidation from 1936 - 1946, it grew rapidly on the West Coast with the preaching of Gerald L. K. Smith. Southern California was the vanguard of this ideology as several of Smith's protégés, including William Gale, preached and expanded upon the Christian Identity doctrine.[148]

Gale founded one of the early Christian Identity militias of the 1960s, the California Rangers. California's Attorney General referred to the Rangers as an underground network for the conduct of guerilla warfare.[149] It was Gale who introduced Richard Butler to Christian Identity leader Wesley Swift in the early 1960s. Later, Butler would leave for northern Idaho, where he would begin to help establish a racially "pure" settlement around Hayden Lake and serve briefly as a mentor to Robert Mathews of the Order.[150]

Though some of the early modern militias could be classified as "constitutional," the predominant ideology of this earlier phase of the movement was based on that of Christian Identity. This was largely due to a popular and influential book (among militia members) by William Pierce called *The Turner Diaries*.[151] The book is a fictional account of a racist, anti-Semitic underground militia that, through a series of violent acts during the 1990s, gains power in America and eventually the world. A key act is the bombing of FBI headquarters in Washington using a truck bomb, and the end result of the overall attack is the "liberation" of the United States and the elimination of its minority population.

Pierce was not Christian Identity, but his book was widely read and admired by many who attended a 1982 meeting of right-wing organizations in northern Idaho, the purpose of which was to sign an Identity-inspired document called the Nehemiah Township Charter and Common Law Contract.[152] Believing that the "Zionist Occupational Government" (i.e., the U.S. federal government) had perverted the U.S. Constitution and the Declaration of Independence and that those two documents were no longer "covenants between God and Man," the Nehemiah Charter was considered the new covenant. It would become the constitution under which the new government would rule after Armageddon. According to the charter, Jesus Christ would lead the new government, whose purpose would be to safeguard and protect the Christian faith. There would be no legislative body, no taxation, and no governmental laws, and only freemen (i.e., whites) would have personal freedoms according to a "Common Law" enforced by Posse Comitatus.[153]

In the neo militia movement of the 1990s (defined as the movement that began in the United States about 1992 and continued until around 2000), some constitutionalist themes are present along with some underlying Christian Identity themes.[154] The literature does not conclusively answer the question of which kind of theme is predominant. Consequently, the question of whether or not the neo-militia flows directly from the white supremacist movement or is something distinctly detached from it is a question that could not be answered from the literature review.

However, the extant literature (some of it admittedly non sociological) provides evidence that Smelser's theory of collective behavior is a potentially adequate frame of reference for studying neo militias. Smelser's general theory accounts for the development of various kinds of collective behavior, social movements being only one type. It is often referred to as one of the classical social movement theories and has one preliminary point followed by five main points.

The preliminary point is that a social structure must be conducive or permissive of a certain kind of collective behavior. A money market, for instance, even though its structure is conducive to panic, may function for long periods without producing a crisis. Within the scope of a conducive structure, many possible kinds of behavior other than panic remain. Similarly, in a free democratic nation such as the United States, the social structure is conducive to many possible kinds of behavior other than radical social movements. To narrow the range of possibilities, Smelser added several more determinants that make it ever more probable that a particular type of collective behavior would emerge.[155]

First, Smelser believed that underlying social strain must be present for a social movement to occur. He defined "strain" as the impairment of the relations among, and consequent inadequate function of, the components of social action.[156] Following Talcott Parsons and Edward Shils, Smelser defined the four components as values, norms, mobilization into organized roles (social structures), and situational facilities (actor's knowledge of the opportunities and limitations of the environment).[157] These are arranged in a hierarchy with values ranked highest and facilities lowest. Furthermore, moving from the top to the bottom of the hierarchy, concrete details of action receive increasingly more specific definition. Smelser believed that strain in a social system will show itself at a lower, more operative level, such as the mobilization into organized roles or situational facilities. Once this strain appears at this lower level, a search for the reasons for the strain begins to call into action the higher levels. Smelser's view was that strain could manifest itself in many ways, strains could cluster together in unusual ways, and the relationships among multiple strains could be complex.[158]

Smelser did see a correlation between certain types of strain and certain types of collective behavior. He notes that value-oriented beliefs (the kind found in a militia movement) may arise under conditions of severe physical deprivation or economic hardship, as was the case in the millenarian movements in the late Middle Ages.[159] Here, the strain is a psychological state of the individual as well as an objective condition that observers can see. Recent research shows a similar link between deprivation and the rise of right-wing activity. Weinberg for example contends that the radical right (including militias) of the 1980s drew members from economically distressed sectors of the economy. Due to global corporate restructuring, the number of employed Americans whose incomes fell below the poverty line rose 23 percent in 1978-1987. The principal losers in this trend, who felt a real decline in their earning power, were those workers engaged in routine production services (e.g., farming, manufacturing) and those who provide routine personal services such as truck drivers, custodians, restaurant employees, and barbers.[160] Adding to this real deprivation was the relative deprivation suffered by some whites as their status in the world was declining relative to other racial categories in society. In particular, there was an undercurrent of resentment against what are seen as the unfair advantages the government gives to people of color and women. In the eyes of these whites, these advantages are the result of the feminist and civil rights movements, civil rights legislation and court decisions, welfare, affirmative action programs, and educational programs for the economically disadvantaged that exclude nonminorities.[161]

There is another kind of strain that correlates with the behavior of radical social movements such as militias. Smelser writes that inadequacy of knowledge or techniques to grapple with new situations sets the stage for the value-oriented movements. Value-oriented beliefs are not a simple function of superstition or lack of knowledge; the inadequacy of facilities to explain unusual events or cope with situational problems does, however, contribute to the rise of these, rather than other types of movements.[162] Daniel Bell for instance wrote that the radical Right of the early 1960s, including some militias, arose due the inability to comprehend "modernity," or the belief in rational assessment, rather than established custom, for the evaluation of social change. Furthermore, this modernity was a bellwether in the fading dominance of custom, once exercised through the institutions of small-town America.[163] Moreover, a similar inability to comprehend "post modernity" in which prior rational assessments were no longer guideposts for understanding rapid social change, may have been important in the rise of the patriot movement and especially the constitutional neo militias of the 1990s.[164] Anthony Giddens further argued that the complexities of postmodern globalization may have led to the development of political and religious fundamentalisms.[165]

Second, Smelser posits a generalized belief that identifies the source of strain and at least suggests certain lines of actions as being appropriate to remedy the source of the strain. This is, in Smelser's terms, the search for an explanation of the source of strain at a higher level of social action, that is, norms and values.[166] Among future militiamen, at least one such generalized belief, the "New World Order," began to circulate in the early 1990s, just before the appearance of the movement.[167] This generalized belief stimulated thoughts about how to contain this new threat and the types of action that might be needed. According to this idea, a U.N.-led force was poised to take over the United States and administer a totalitarian, collectivist government.[168] Fear of collectivism was the militias' "call to arms," and devotees thought that they must bear arms and train to resist an impending takeover.[169]

Third, Smelser contended that hastening or precipitating events must confirm the generalized belief before the movement can appear. These events create, sharpen, or exaggerate a condition of strain and link the generalized belief to concrete situations. By doing so, a movement becomes closer to actualization. The perceived heavy-handed treatment of U.S. citizens by government agents in Ruby Ridge, Idaho, and Waco, Texas, reinforced the imagery of the New World Order and, according to some, helped precipitate the neo militia movement.[170] At Ruby Ridge, Randy Weaver had been indicted for selling illegal shotguns to an informant and refused to appear in court. This led to a tense, controversial standoff between Weaver and a force of U.S. marshals, FBI and ATF agents, during which Weaver's wife Vicki and son Sammy were shot and killed. At Waco, a raid by ATF agents at the compound of a religious sect called the Branch Davidians resulted in a shootout followed by a fifty-one-day standoff. This standoff ended with a fire in which seventy-six Branch Davidians died.

Fourth, Smelser believed that leaders emerge to give the fledgling movement a sense of direction. He believed, following Max Weber, that leaders in a value-oriented movement such as a militia would be charismatic, with exceptional powers or qualities.[171] Because a value-oriented movement calls for a reconstruction of the entire social order, a diffuse, total kind of commitment is needed. Charismatic leadership is, then, the most generalized form of leadership, for in such a leader is placed the hopes for a collective reconstitution of values.[172] Several charismatic leaders (e.g., Bob Fletcher, Bo Gritz, J. J. Johnson, Martin Lindstedt, and Linda Thompson) played a role in mobilizing the neo militia movement and, along the way, demonstrated a sophisticated use of the Internet as a tool to assist in movement mobilization.[173]

Finally, social control mechanisms initiated by elites in power affect the direction of the movement once it has started. Smelser believed that a value-oriented movement, once crystallized, has a potential for moving in many directions: it may come to naught; it may form into a cult or a sect; it may go underground; or it may turn into a revolutionary force. A major determinant of the movement's course lies in the behavior of agencies of social control in response to the movement. According to some analysts, the official response to the militia movement in the United States in the form of anti terrorism legislation as well as negative press drove a significant proportion of the movement underground, one of the possibilities suggested by Smelser.[174]

The studies cited in this section to support the application of Smelser's theory to neo militias are secondary sources. Thus, a summary statement would be that Smelser's theory is supported by secondary sources but has yet to be tested with primary data with respect to the militia phenomenon in the United States.

Several competing theories rose to challenge Smelser's. Resource mobilization theory (developed mostly to overcome perceived weaknesses in the social strain approach) emphasizes that social movements should be seen as rational, goal-oriented efforts to engage in political conflict for realistic advantages. According to this view, protests may be the only way in which groups excluded from established institutions can fight effectively for their interests. Strain may not be necessary in these circumstances, in that there are always social strains and conflicts of interest built into existing social arrangements. But often less powerful groups are too atomized or demoralized to form a social movement. Thus, this approach emphasizes the element of time that it takes for atomized or disconnected aggrieved people to form associations with one another. For resource mobilization theorists, potentially aggrieved groups must achieve some degree of solidarity in order to act; and preexisting social networks or organizations are likely to be involved in launching social movements.[175]

Another alternative, Marxist theories, argues that the formation of social movements is tied to capitalist social structure.[176] The work of Robert Reich points out how even at the higher reaches of the pay scale there is economic stress due to job insecurity, declining wages, and additional hours worked.[177] This argument points toward a progressive slide of the seemingly well off into a Marxian "working class" and implies, at least, that a two-class model has some viability in explaining a phenomenon such as the militias, whose membership is believed to be predominantly middle class.[178] Threats to well-being need not be purely economic but may be psychological as well. Thus, one might be able to argue that the militias are indeed a “class” phenomenon and do have middle - or working class interests diametrically opposed to a ruling class in a two-class system.

Doug McAdam’s political opportunities model tried to tap the strengths but also improve upon the weaknesses of both the classical and resource mobilization approaches. It is a process model, like Smelser's, and is also concerned with the degree to which organizations are ready and able to provide support for a movement. The political process model identifies three sets of factors that are believed to be crucial in the generation of social insurgency. The first is the level of organization within the aggrieved population (degree of organizational "readiness"); the second is the collective assessment of the prospects for successful insurgency within that same population (level of "insurgent consciousness" within the mass base of the movement); and the third is the political alignment of groups within the larger political environment (the structure of political opportunities available to insurgent groups).[179] The concern with degree of readiness of insurgent groups reflects the concern with the time element that is explicit in resource mobilization theory as well as the importance that preexisting networks may play in this process.

David Snow, E. Burke Rochford, Steven Worden, and Robert Benford have taken a different track, choosing to refine and extend our understanding of the cognitive basis of collective action by proposing a typology of "frame alignment processes" that activists use to construct legitimating accounts to support their own and others' activism.[180] New movements always entail some break with established behavioral routines. In order to overcome people's natural reluctance to break with these routines, ideological rationales must be fashioned that legitimate the movement's behavioral proscriptions. Snow and his colleagues distinguish four distinct frame alignment processes -- frame bridging, frame amplification, frame extension, and frame transformation -- by which these rationales are constructed.

Despite the worthy and viable alternative theories to choose from, we continue to believe that Smelser's framework has potential utility in explaining and predicting militia behavior. His theory provides a good match with the available secondary source information, and it provides a theoretically grounded, logical, and temporal explanation for the appearance of the militia movement. Furthermore, if the theory is validated by primary data, it could assist social scientists in predicting the next wave of militia activity.

Methods and Data

Smelser's theory was tested in this study by analyzing the content of Internet traffic of U.S. neo militias. This includes a content analysis of Web pages and Usenet traffic. Each message or page was scrutinized carefully for both its manifest and latent content.[181] Content analysis as a research design has the advantage of allowing the researcher the opportunity to peruse the message an unlimited number of times, whereas in observational studies or interviews, the observer's memory and note-taking skills are called into play as key variables in the data gathering process. Additionally, an unobtrusive study of Internet traffic avoids the problem of reactivity that might be expected in studying militiamen and women.

A citizen militia is conceptually defined the same as a private army: it meets regularly to practice combat scenarios or skills and to discuss weapons. It may identify targets against which weapons could be used, and may carry out missions. A citizen militia may have an offensive, paramilitary orientation (seek and destroy) or a defensive orientation (e.g., protecting America from the New World Order) or both, depending upon circumstances.[182] Operationally, a citizen militia is defined as a group that (1) puts combat scenarios/skills and weaponry plans into (at least) mock action, including "maneuvers," (2) has an identifiable territory in which its members reside, (3) bases its organizational philosophies on anti-government rhetoric, (4) develops contingency plans in case of government provocation, (5) considers (at least) the viability of extreme measures to protect the organic constitution and/or white race such as bombing, kidnappings, separatism, and "paper terrorism," and (6) considers (at least) the viability of criminal activity to acquire weapons and explosives.[183] This definition indicates that militias are social groups that practice skills within a distinct territory, are anti-government in outlook, and have definite opinions regarding use of terrorism to further militia goals.

The data for this study were drawn from a preliminary list of 244 militias identified during August 1998 from a number of sources: the Southern Poverty Law Center, John Whitley, and a systematic browsing of the Internet, the *New York Times Index*, and First Search.[184] The final list of militias to be studied was determined by screening each of the militias on the preliminary list against the operational definition of a citizen militia as it is defined in this study. Each militia that met the operational definition was checked to see if it had a Web site or if it had generated a significant amount of Usenet traffic. This procedure identified 28 militias in five regions of the United States. A total of 171 militiamen/women were studied who belonged to the 28 identified militias. Each research subject was assigned a case number; all but one can be identified by name.

Of the 28 militias studied, 7 were from the Southeast, 9 from the West, 7 from the Midwest, 3 from the Southwest, and 2 from the East. Of the militiamen and women who belonged to these militias, 19 were from the Southeast, 33 were from the West, 42 were from the Midwest, 69 were from the Southwest, and 8 were from the East. Compared with a group of 133 militias studied by the Southern Poverty Law Center, our sample is slightly overrepresented with militias from the West and is under represented by Midwestern and Eastern militias.[185]

Nearly all the subjects were men (97 percent), and, though data on ethnic group identity was not generally available nor could be inferred from most messages posted, we do know that at least two subjects are African American and one is Jewish. The remainder is probably white, based on an examination of subjects' surnames together with the observations about ethnicity made by the "watch" organizations.[186] Occupational data was available for 54 of the militiamen or women. This is self-reported data as well as data that are reported by militia leaders or occupations attributed to militiamen or women by their peers. We have no reason to believe that this data is any more or less reliable than other kinds of self-reported occupational data. Professionals or managerial workers accounted for 33.3 percent of the total; sales, technical, and administrative for 37 percent; manual labor for 24.1 percent; and low skill and service workers made up 5.6 percent of the total. Leaders accounted for 19 percent of the total subjects studied and followers were 81 percent.

All research subjects had access to Usenet, a discussion system that is distributed worldwide. It consists of a set of news groups with names that are classified by subject. Messages are "posted" to these news groups by people with the appropriate software and access to the Internet. Consequently, Usenet is not a bulletin board, listserv, or "chat line." The Usenet archive, *Deja News*, saved all messages posted until being taken over by Google in February 2001. Most subjects signed their names to the messages. Therefore, we were able to sort through all the messages for each subject to observe writing styles and message content, and it was very obvious when an imposter tried to claim the identity of one of the regular posters, given the vehement negative response of that regular poster. We actually got to "know" the people through their messages and style of presentation, and we felt that enough of a paper trail was left that we could state that these were real militiamen or women with strong convictions. Additionally, many of these individuals were already publicly identified by "watch" organizations or by public proclamations on Usenet announcing regional leaders of some of the militias studied. This further supports the idea that the militiamen and women were actual people and not anonymous individuals posting and then leaving the newsgroup. Thus, the question, "Who are these people?" is not an issue. All but one can be identified by name. The real issue is how the names of these subjects can be kept confidential. While it cannot be verified beyond a reasonable doubt that each and every message posted was posted by a militiaman or woman (and not a federal agent, scholar, extremist watcher, or other interested party), the high volume of messages posted by many subjects together with the highly emotional content of several of the messages would appear to weigh against the probability that participation is based purely upon those pecuniary or professional considerations that might be the top priority of an agent who is infiltrating the group.

Several questions could be raised about the representativeness of the sample. Does this study look at a socioeconomically more affluent subset of the militia movement because it is limited to militiamen/women who own a computer and have the technological capability to post to the Internet? This would suggest a higher level of intelligence and possibly more income than other militiamen or women. Thus, are the message posters truly representative of a broader group of militia members who may or may not use the Internet? Is the Internet user group a unique subset of all militia members, a distinctive set of leaders, or more typical of the "average" militia member?

Evidence suggests that many who joined militias in the 1990s already had computer competency due to their participation in computer bulletin board systems or BBS. A BBS is a freestanding computer system that is tied to one or more phone lines. Dial-in users can exchange text files and messages. Virtually anyone with a computer, modem, and phone line could hook up to the bulletin board. Technological savvy was not required, nor was state of the art equipment; old, second-hand equipment, which could be purchased at pawnshops, was entirely adequate. Moreover, some of the bulletin board systems were quite popular en masse. The Paul Revere Network that began in 1987 connected thousands of patriots as did Liberty Net, Patriot Net, Spirit of '76, Associated Electronic News, and other bulletin boards. The mass strength of these patriot networks was first evident during the 1992 presidential campaign of independent Ross Perot. Libertarians and populist conservatives, who appear to have strongly influenced the politics of early cyber-culture and later the Internet, helped circulate organizing documents and position papers for the Perot campaign, quickly reaching a large audience. Perot's anti government themes also attracted support from some persons in the extremist Right who later went on to promote the patriot and militia movements.[187] According to Chip Berlet, these pre existing on-line relationships were a factor in the subsequent use of computer networks by the patriot and militia movements. A large amount of information and numerous discussions about tactics and strategy for the militia and patriot movements moved across the Internet, appearing in Usenet newsgroup conferences such as alt.conspiracy, talk.politics.guns, alt.sovereignty, misc.survivalism, alt.politics.usa.constitution, and ultimately, misc.activism.militia.[188] In short, those who were posting to militia Usenet groups by the mid-1990s, both leaders and rank and file, had been plugged in to computers for about ten years. Their participation was more a matter of ideological commitment than of occupation, income, or technical knowledge.

Relevant information from Web sites and Usenet postings by or about the selected militias and militiamen was downloaded to diskettes from September 1, 1998, to August 22, 2001. Overall, 6,285 on-line documents were downloaded for analysis. Of these, 1,196 had sufficient content to answer one or more of the research questions. Because one document could have information relevant to more than one research question, there are a total of 1,249 messages that were related to the six research questions posed in this study.

The downloaded information was converted to Microsoft Word files, then Nonnumerical Unstructured Data Indexing Searching and Theorizing (NUDIST) was used to assist with the data analysis.[189] This software package was programmed to look for keywords and chunks of text (the sentences prior to and after the keyword) that pertain to the six research questions; it then generated a report related to each keyword.

These reports indicated the files that might be germane to each of the research questions. Each file was then checked and each document that helped to answer any of the research questions was examined for its manifest and latent content and coded according to instructions that appeared in the codebook of the principal investigator. Smelser's theory would be considered falsified if there were little or no evidence to answer any one of the research questions.

Variables and Research Questions

Figure 1 provides a visual overview of Smelser's theory. The preliminary point is not tested here because freedom of speech and assembly is guaranteed in the U.S. Constitution, and thus the U.S. social structure is conducive to the development of citizen militias and other kinds of social movements. Second, there is structural conduciveness because of the structure of computer bulletin boards that allow for open communication and set the stage for the development of the militias utilizing the Internet as an organizing tool. The discussion below documents the remaining variables and research questions.

Structural Strain. Smelser notes that structural strain is a precondition for the development of a social movement. Considering that extremist watchers have identified strains similar to those mentioned by Smelser,[190] the question to be answered is: Did militiamen/women experience strain prior to or during their tenure in the militia?

Smelser delineated four types of strain that he believed would be most common as a precondition for a social movement; however, he eventually conceded that any kind of strain can produce any kind of movement. Consequently, we made the decision here to include any kinds of strains that might be reported by or for militiamen or women.

Generalized Beliefs. According to Smelser, strain alone was not sufficient for a social movement to appear; it must be accompanied by at least one generalized belief that puts the participant's stress into a context and gives an explanation for the kinds of stress being experienced. Given that the literature documents the appearance of a belief called the New World Order,[191] the relevant question is: Before or after joining the militia, were militiamen or women introduced to the idea of the New World Order, and did they accept it?

In this study, messages whose manifest and latent content indicated that the militiaman or woman had accepted the concept of the New World Order prior to or during militia membership were coded as indicating support for that particular generalized belief. This includes explicit remarks by individuals that indicate acceptance of the New World Order or support as inferred from individual remarks and group statements or declarations. Nonsupport for the New World Order was noted in militia messages where there was no acceptance of this generalized belief as a frame of reference for understanding the kinds of stress experienced. This includes explicit remarks that this belief is not important (e.g., "we do not think about the NWO, this is an urban myth perpetuated by the media"), or explicit comments that other kinds of concepts may be more important (e.g., instead of militias being concerned with NWO, "most are mainly concerned with getting the federal government down to a manageable size"), or the same result as inferred from remarks posted (e.g., the Alabama Declaration that was signed by several militiamen and women in support of constitutionalist principles contains no references at all to NWO).

Figure 1. Overview of Smelser's Theory of Collective Behavior

Preliminary Point	A social structure must be conducive or permissive of a certain kind of collective behavior or social movement.
Major Point 1	Underlying social strain must be present for a social movement to occur.
Major Point 2	At least one generalized belief must appear that identifies the source of strain and suggests certain lines of action as being appropriate to remedy the source of the strain.
Major Point 3	Precipitating events must confirm the generalized belief before the movement can appear.
Major Point 4	Leaders engage in a mobilization for action that gives the fledgling movement a sense of direction.
Major Point 5	Social control mechanisms initiated by elites in power affects the direction of the movement once it has started. A value-oriented movement has potential to move in many directions: it may come to naught; it may form into a cult or a sect; it may go underground; or it may turn into a revolutionary force.

Precipitating Events. The existence of strain accompanied by generalized beliefs is not enough to produce an episode of collective behavior, according to Smelser. Precipitating events are crucial. These events confirm the explanations for stress contained within the generalized belief and crystallize calls for action. Some writers contend that certain important events precipitated the rise of the neo-militia movement,[192] so the research question is: Were events at Ruby Ridge and Waco, together with the passage of gun control legislation, important reasons for participants to join the militia?

Mobilization for Action. Given the appearance of strain, generalized beliefs, and precipitating events, there is still a possibility that no social movement will emerge, unless there is a mobilization for action in which certain key individuals take the lead.[193] Because it has been suggested that the Internet provided a platform for leaders to move quickly to mobilize the movement,[194] the "mobilization for action" variable was concerned with the type of specific media that the militiamen believed was most helpful in mobilizing the movement. The specific research question that relates to this variable is: Did the Internet play a more important role than other media in helping to mobilize the movement?

Social Control. Social control, to Smelser, refers to the mechanisms that affect the direction of a movement once it has begun. It is the sum total of mechanisms that disrupt or inhibit a movement in progress, rather than social control in the sense of enforcing norms.[195] Here, we are primarily concerned with the electronic implications of the Oklahoma City bombing and specifically, from an electronic standpoint, if social control tactics led to an abandonment of Internet traffic for more secure kinds of communications such as encrypted e-mail messages or the confidential communications within small leaderless cells.[196] The related research question is: Following the Oklahoma City bombing, did social control influence movement participants to use the Internet less and "underground" kinds of communications more often? This variable was measured by traffic as recorded in the Usenet archive "*Deja News*."

Orientation. An important question unresolved in previous literature – and an issue unrelated to Smelser's theory – is the issue of the ideological orientation of the neo militia movement. There is a difference of opinion among writers who stress the constitutionalism of the militias and those who believe that Christian Identity beliefs underlie most militia rhetoric.[197] Therefore, in this study, the variable, "orientation" is concerned with whether the primary ideology of the militia, or at least that of the individual posting the message, is primarily constitutionalist or primarily Christian Identity. The related research question is: What is the primary orientation of the movement, constitutionalist or Christian Identity?

Messages with constitutionalist content pointed to the New World Order or other generalized belief and the need to train and bear arms to resist a collectivist takeover. Christian Identity messages stressed the militia as an all-Aryan body, upholders of true Israelism, with an uncompromising stance with respect to religious beliefs, and spoke of a final war against the "forces of darkness," that is, nonwhite opponents and their allies.[198]

Results and Discussion

Table 8 shows that there were indeed multiple strains upon militiamen/women prior to joining the militia, or during militia membership. Nine types of strain were identified, the most important of which were indicated by the militiamen as fear of the United States federal government. Over 63 percent of the messages related to the first question expressed this fear of the government. Within this 63 percent, 30 percent feared that federal and/or international police forces were growing in power; 20 percent mentioned a fear of government without elaborating in more detail; and 13 percent felt that the federal government with its harsh and repressive policies was becoming more like the former Soviet Union. A militiaman who was fearful of the growing power of U.S. federal police posted this message about this particular strain:

> Experts who have been watching such developments say all this is leading one place--to the establishment of a genuine national police force. You can see it in the way the FBI now routinely interferes in local law enforcement affairs. You can also see it in the plans of big-government architects . . . who [have] urged that Treasury Department police agencies ....

> … be placed under the control of the Justice Department.[199]

Another militiaman, fearing the "Sovietization" of U.S. police forces, expressed the following: "I am scared that we are becoming a police state a la Nazi Germany or Stalinist Russia. I do not want to be slave labor."[200]

The remaining 37 percent of the responses were as follows: 8 percent indicated that they experienced economic distress; 6 percent had experienced rapid social changes; 6 percent said that their standard of living was declining; 6 percent said that globalization had affected them, or that they had lost their jobs; 6 percent indicated a distrust of government or a discontent with it; and 5 percent listed strains other than those mentioned above.

The fear of the federal government that we found in this study has also been documented by other researchers who, like Smelser, agree that is a precondition for the growth of the neo militia movement.[201] As militiamen in this study described it, this fear centers on the unchecked growth and power of the federal government and its tendency to develop a federal policing model that resembles that of the former Soviet Union. If it is different than fears articulated in previous studies, it is because militiamen here seemed reluctant to mention specific issues of a personal nature that other militiamen had mentioned to other researchers, for instance, the fear that government agents and/or police will interfere in private family matters (divorce, custody battles), may over regulate their businesses resulting in financial ruin, may confiscate weapons, or may take away freedom of religion.

Data in Table 9 correspond to the second research question: Before joining the militia, or during militia membership, were militiamen or women introduced to the idea of the New World Order, and did they accept it? The data indicate that there was no significant difference in the number of militiamen who accepted or did not accept the concept of the New World Order prior to or during their membership in the militia. Case number 42, a strong advocate for the idea of the New World Order, said that militia wrath is centered on the United Nations because it is controlled by an alliance between big business and the Soviet Union, who are intent upon destroying America and creating a New World Order.[202] Like many others, this person clearly accepted the notion of the NWO.

Interestingly, over 48 percent of the militiamen for whom information was available reported that they had not been introduced to the New World Order prior to joining the militia, or during militia membership or, if introduced to the idea, did not accept it. Some had become familiar instead with the Zionist Occupational Government or ZOG. This is similar to the New World Order idea. ZOG is the “Jewish-controlled” U.S. federal government that is trying to impose a one-world socialist government. Another alternative could be called "police state." This idea is basically that law enforcement at all levels is abusive, corrupt, and exercising executive powers well beyond its mandate. As one advocate put it:

> I was . . . outraged when government forces firebombed an inner city neighborhood of Philadelphia in 1985, killing 11 . . . and then there are the countless murders and cover-ups by "law enforcement" that have become common-place in my community.[203]

Other militiamen simply did not accept the idea of the NWO and clearly did not think it was important. Two of the militiamen responded:

> "New World Order" is probably not the term used by the shadow government to refer to their strategic plan. It appears to have been invented by conspiracy theorists, and its use detracts from our credibility.[204]

> We do not think about the NWO; this is an urban myth perpetuated by the media.[205]

Table 8. Structural Strain Reported by/for U.S. Militiamen/Women

Strain Reported	% of Relevant Messages
Fear federal/global police force	30.4 (38)
Fear federal government	20.0 (25)
Fear U.S. "Soviet" state	12.8 (16)
Economic distress (unspecified)	8.0 (10)
Rapid social change	6.4 (8)
Shrinking standard of living	6.4 (8)
Globalization or job loss	5.6 (7)
Distrust of or discontent with government	5.6 (7)
Other	4.8 (6)
Total	100.0

Note:
Number of Relevant messages = 125

Table 9. Militiamen/Women Accepting Concept of New World Order Before/During Militia Membership

	% of Relevant Messages
Accepted NWO Concept	51.8 (57)
Did Not Accept NWO Concept (rejected NWO or accepted an alternative belief such as ZOG or police state)	48.2 (53)
Total	100.00

Notes:
Data not available for 61 of the militiamen or women. Militiamen/women reporting = 110; Number of Relevant messages = 110

After data collection, a further review of relevant literature did reveal the existence of competing generalized beliefs (e.g., ZOG, police state) and evidence that some militiamen/women simply did not believe in the New World Order.[206] Smelser did not specify that one and only one generalized belief occurred with the onset of each new social movement. More than one could be present, and he referred to five different types. One of these, the hostile belief, is salient to the neo militias. It is salient not only to the New World Order but also to the other generalized beliefs uncovered in the study. The hostile belief identifies the source of strain, seeks to mobilize to attack this agent, and exaggerates the power to remove the source of evil.[207] Hence, in the case of the NWO or ZOG, it is this "evil beast" that is the source and the force driving the involvement of U.S. governmental agents into the private lives of American citizens. It, the beast, is the source of America's slide into collectivism, rather than the government or its agents per se. This allows the militiamen and women to remain true U.S. patriots, committed to the U.S. Constitution without being anti-American.

According to Smelser, mobilization of arms to protect citizens from attack becomes the suggested means of coping with this agent, and there is "wishful thinking" that these mobilized groups can actually gather up the power to remove the source of evil.[208]

The third research question asked if events at Ruby Ridge and Waco together with gun control legislation were the most important precipitating events that prompted individuals to join militias or to remain in them. According to Table 10, Waco and Ruby Ridge were the most frequently mentioned precipitants of the U.S. neo-militia movement. These two events were mentioned by 77 percent of the individuals posting a message relevant to this research question. On the other hand, the Brady Bill was mentioned in only 11 percent of the messages and the Assault Weapons Bill of 1994 was mentioned in only 6 percent of the messages. A 1992 meeting at Estes Park, Colorado, believed by some writers to be an important catalyst of the militia movement, was mentioned in only 2 percent of the relevant messages.

There is substantial corroborating documentation that these two events are the primary precipitants of the movement.[209] The future militiamen and women - those studied here as well as those in other studies - wondered why so much federal firepower was allocated for Weaver, living in a dilapidated shed in an isolated part of Idaho with his wife and family, and for the Branch Dividians, a small and unpopular religious sect. These militia individuals were deeply troubled by the raw force that led to loss of life at Ruby Ridge and Waco.[210] These two events therefore became powerful symbols of an out-of-control federal government, that was intent on NWO or ZOG, and that would stop at nothing to impose its will upon helpless citizens. Extremist watchers promoted the idea that weapons legislation was an important precipitant, but the data in this study did not support this contention. The brute force exercised at Waco and Ruby Ridge confirmed the generalized beliefs in a more complete way than any group of weapons bills could possibly confirm, based on the Internet messages studied.

To answer the fourth research question (Table 11) concerning the importance of the Internet in helping to mobilize the movement, 48 percent of the messages indicate Internet, Usenet, or computer bulletin boards as the preferred media compared with only 21 percent that preferred faxes. Though a number of other media were mentioned less frequently (shortwave radio, talk shows, cable TV, videos, e-mail, direct mail), messages stressed that the media were not in competition with one another but were, when taken as a whole, a credible alternative source of information and much preferred overall to the mainstream media.

Results of Table 12 (corresponding to question five) show that Usenet, a public form of communication, was used with increasing frequency after the Oklahoma City bombing. Smelser's theory suggested that forcing a movement "underground" was one of the possible outcomes of social control, and the literature review suggests that many groups had gone underground. Thus, there was a reasonable expectation that Usenet traffic might decline over time. Instead, the number of messages posted to three militia-oriented news groups by or about the 171 militiamen increased from 2,186 during a twenty-month period immediately after the bombing, to 3,595 in a comparable period in 1997-1998, a 64 percent increase. This occurred despite evidence in eighty messages that many militias went underground after the bombing and engaged in more secure kinds of communications: computer bulletin boards, encrypted e-mail, heavily coded messages, and the confidential talk of leaderless cells.

Table 10. Precipitants of U.S. Militia Movement Mentioned by or for U.S. Militiamen/Women

Event	% of Relevant Messages	
Waco	40.6	(136)
Ruby Ridge	36.1	(121)
Brady Bill	11.3	(38)
Assault Weapons Bill	6.0	(20)
Estes Park meeting	2.1	(7)
Other (LA Riot, MOVE, Desert Storm)	2.1	(7)
G.H.W. Bush's NWO Speech (1990)	1.8	(6)
Total	100.0	

Note:
Relevant messages = 335.

Table 11. Media of Choice Reported by/for U.S. Militiamen/Women

Media	% of Relevant Messages	
Bulletin boards/Usenet/Internet	48.0	(71)
FAX	20.9	(31)
Short wave radio	11.5	(17)
Talk shows/cable TV/videos	7.4	(11)
E-mail	6.1	(9)
Direct mail	6.1	(9)
Total	100.0	

Note:
Relevant messages = 148.

The growth in militia traffic on the Internet following the Oklahoma City bombing has been noted elsewhere in the research literature.[211] This trend would appear to support the view that militia membership grew after and in spite of the bombing. However, John George and Laird Wilcox offer the opposite view. They contend that many militiamen and women dropped out after the bombing (due to the FBI hotline on tips to the bombing) and as mentioned earlier, some our messages confirm this.[212] Given these conflicting interpretations, the growth in Internet traffic deserves careful study.

How can we account for the growth in this traffic, especially at a time when there is evidence that militia membership was declining? A number of explanations are feasible. First, we know that Internet traffic grew because militiamen utilized Usenet as an acceptable alternative media that was relatively free from censoring. Second, a number of militia controversies were reported in the mainstream press; later, a "correct" interpretation and coverage appeared in the mostly unfiltered Usenet messages.[213] Third, by 1996 the movement was beginning to splinter, which contributed to the traffic by adding controversial topics for discussion as well as longer discussion threads. For example, case 83 broke from the constitutionalists and joined the Christian Identity faction. He engaged in some long and bitter threads with his former constitutionalist peers. Then, a common law faction and an anti militia faction (including ex-militiamen) engaged in some bitter debates with both constitutionalists and Christian Identity. These discussions added to the increase in traffic in the militia-oriented newsgroups.

Is it possible that the increase on the three discussion groups is simply a reflection of an overall increased interest in the Internet as a means of communication? To test this idea we would need to look at the total traffic on several different types newsgroups during the two time frames we are studying. Ideally we would have compared the traffic on the three militia-oriented groups with three mainstream discussion groups, for example, those of the Democratic, Republican, and Reform parties. Due to the demise of the superior search engine "*Deja News*" in February 2001, such comparisons are unfortunately no longer possible.

However, we can compare the numbers of militia postings on the three news groups studied with the total traffic on those newsgroups. As Table 13 shows, the overall traffic, which included militia and nonmilitia messages, increased in all three news groups by 111 percent overall. Perhaps unexpectedly, we found that the militia postings were only about 3–4 percent of the total postings, if we compare the results of Table 12 with Table 13. This indicates that a huge percentage of posters to the militia-oriented news groups cover a wide range of people who have some interest in militias but a very large contingent who do not belong to any militia. Hence, the posters ranged from people with a casual curiosity about militias, to militia "wannabes," to serious and active militia members who were having event-focused, specific dialogues with one another. The nonmilitia traffic, which we perused occasionally, reflected great diversity: it consisted of (among others) (1) "reluctant" posters who were sympathetic but could not join a militia for some reason, (2) derogatory, flaming messages critical of militias in general, or (3)

Table 12. Growth in Usenet Traffic on Three Militia-Oriented News Groups (Militia Traffic Only)

News Group	Number of Messages Posted from: 4-20-95 to 12-31-96	1-1-97 to 9-11-98	% Increase/Decrease
Misc-Activism-Militia	1444	2864	+98.0
Talk-Politics-Guns (a)	542	596	+10.0
Misc-Survivalism	200	135	-33.0
Total	2186	3595	+64.0

Notes:

This is traffic by or about the 28 militias studied; this is the "militia traffic" only.

(a) Using the "*Deja News*" power search function, the archive was checked for messages that included the term "militia." Only those messages that had content relevant to the militias were reviewed. This procedure effectively screened out messages that were not militia-related.

Table 13. Growth in Usenet Traffic on Three Militia-Oriented News Groups (All Traffic)

News Group	Number of Messages Posted from: 4-20-95 to 12-31-96	1-1-97 to 9-11-98	% Increase/Decrease
Misc-Activism-Militia	41811	81978	+96.0
Talk-Politics-Guns (a)	7642	23027	+201.0
Misc-Survivalism	808	1174	+45.0
Total	50,261	106,179	+111.0

Notes:

This is *all* the traffic in the newsgroup, both militia and nonmilitia.

(a) Using the "*Deja News*" power search function, the archive was checked for messages that included the term "militia." Only those messages that had content relevant to the militias were reviewed. This procedure effectively screened out messages that were not militia-related.

Table 14. Primary Orientations Reported by/for U.S. Militiamen/Women

Primary Orientation	% of Relevant Messages
Constitutionalist	65.0 (345)
Christian Identity	35.0 (186)
Total	100.0

Note:
Relevant messages = 531.

cross-talk, that is, messages that were simply cross- posted to several news groups at once. The fact that militia traffic is so small and did not increase as fast, suggests that more factors may be at work than simply the overall increase in volume. We cannot conclude that the increase in militia traffic was simply "riding the coattails" of a general increased interest in the Internet.

Smelser believed that social control would influence the direction of a movement once it starts. The neo militia movement is one example of this phenomenon, at least according to the messages studied. Social control drove some militias underground, as eighty messages suggested, but apparently not completely out of the public domain. They were still able to reach and influence other militiamen or potential militia recruits via the Internet and to argue their case against their antagonists. Thus, while social control played a role in the direction of the movement, that specific direction was not the one suggested by the bulk of the literature review. Most of the reviewed literature suggested that militias would go underground and "drop out," abandoning public forums such as the Internet. Social control also led to the adoption of tactics that could not easily have been predicted as the movement began. Several messages suggested that "leaderless resistance" in small self-contained cells is the model of a militia that goes underground.[214] This redirection of the movement, with an emphasis upon impenetrability, is also something that Smelser's theory suggests.

Data in Table 14, corresponding to the sixth research question, reveal that 65 percent of the relevant messages indicated that the purpose of the militia is to further constitutionalist aims, while 35 percent indicated that the militia's purpose is to further Christian Identity goals. Individual militiamen who composed messages portraying a constitutionalist orientation often went out of their way to separate themselves ideologically from Christian Identity militiamen, and vice versa. A militiaman whose message was representative of the constitutionalist orientation is as follows:

> the bulk of the . . . militias of the various United States have formed a grass roots response to . . . government-sponsored terrorism as well as the continued degradation of constitutional rights at the hands of the current federal administration.[215]

A Christian Identity militiaman posted this incendiary message for his former constitutionalist allies to read:

> Frankly [you Constitutionalists] hate White People. You really hate those of us fighting to restore White America for White People.[216]

Other researchers have confirmed what appears to be the constitutionalist bent of the current movement.[217] In the current study, about two-thirds of the messages posted related to the question about ideology indicated content supportive of constitutionalism. The remaining one-third had content indicative of Christian Identity. While it is difficult to make the bold statement that most militia men and women are constitutionalists based on a limited number of Internet messages, the two-to-one ratio in the messages mirrors those estimates made by extremist watchers and even some militiamen concerning the actual proportion of movement members who are constitutionalists or Christian Identity.[218]

Conclusion

Smelser's theory of collective behavior was selected as the theoretical frame of reference because extant literature about U.S. neo militias indicates that structural strain and other factors specified by Smelser played a role in the genesis and direction of the movement. In general, this study suggests that Smelser's theory adequately explains the emergence and maintenance of the recent militia movement. Figure 2 shows that there is empirical support for Smelser's preliminary point and for four of the five major points. Furthermore, considering that other researchers have confirmed many of the results found here, Smelser's model would appear to have some predictive power and may assist social scientists in predicting the next wave of militia activity. Seymour Lipset and Earl Raub contend that right-wing activity has reappeared at regular intervals throughout U.S. history.[219] Thus, we have reason to believe that the movement is not currently dead, but in abeyance.[220]

Smelser's model predicts that as long as there is strain, generalized beliefs, precipitating events, and a mobilization for action, there will be another wave of militia activity. We have very little evidence at present that the fears underlying the movement have dissipated or that the generalized beliefs within the movement have lost their power as explanations of the stress being experienced. We see progress being made in the prevention of precipitating events. Following the Oklahoma City bombing, an unlikely alliance developed between the FBI, selected militias, and academics at Michigan State University.[221] This alliance may have played a role in defusing the Freeman standoff in Montana and several other potential flashpoints. However, Smelser's model also suggests that some permanent structure of dialogue may be necessary to reduce fears and to forestall the possibility of future precipitants. Specifically, a permanent, structured dialogue based on mutual trust is needed between militiamen and women and the local communities in which they live, and particularly those in positions of such as sheriffs, city councils members, community advisory panel members, county boards of supervisors, and others.[222] These locals, untainted by the far-off villains suggested by the generalized beliefs, are in the best position to allow the militias a forum to vent their grievances and to begin to have a modicum of faith restored in contemporary democratic processes.

Only a small proportion--about 19 percent--of the total documents downloaded to disks, were examined in detail for this study. The remainder had no relevance that we could see to Smelser's theory. This would suggest that there is ample data that could be used to test alternative theories. For example, how did the neo militia movement develop relative to the changing opportunity structures and organizational resources available to it? What framing tasks are revealed in the data? The messages could be treated as texts representing the frames used by members to legitimate their cause; this analysis could proceed without having to deal with the issue of the subject's previous or current psychological states, as one must inevitably do with Smelser's theory. In other words, it would not matter if someone who identifies a particular episode as the "precipitating event" for their joining was actually their own precipitant or if they are simply adopting the rhetoric used by other people in their group. More important would be the rhetoric itself and the framing tasks used. As David Snow and Robert Benford suggest, at least three core framing tasks might be relevant to the militia (and other) movements: (1) a diagnosis of some event or aspect of social life as problematic and in need of alteration, (2) a proposed solution to the diagnosed problem that specifies what needs to be done, and (3) a call to arms or rationale for engaging in ameliorative action.[223] This chapter has suggested that Internet data can be a viable source of information about militias, so a considerable amount of future militia research on the Internet could advance along the lines of frame analysis, political process, and other models competing with Smelser's.

We continue to believe, however, that Smelser's theory is a powerful explanation for the rise of the neo militia movement in the United States. It provides a theoretically grounded, logical, and temporal rationale for the appearance of the movement. It is a good match with much of the available secondary source material. Most important, it is mostly empirically confirmed by the data collected in this study. Only the final component of the theory, social control, was but partially confirmed. Social control influenced the movement but not in the specific direction that much of the secondary source material had suggested. Several reasons were given to account for this finding. This is not a reason to reject the theory. In a way, the final component is the least important to Smelser's theory because it occurs after the genesis of the movement.

Figure 2. Summary of Variables, Measurement, and Results

Variable	.Measured?	How Measured?	Comment or Results
Structural Conduciveness (Preliminary Point)	No	---	U.S. social structure conducive to militia development by constitutional guarantees and by a virtually unregulated forum of communication
Structural Strain (Major Point 1)	Yes	Militia Web pages and Usenet messages	Nine types of strain reported in 125 total messages (Table 8)
Generalized Beliefs (Major Point 2)	Yes	Militia Web pages and Usenet messages	Three beliefs reported in a total of 110 messages (Table 9)
Precipitating Events (Major Point 3)	Yes	Militia Web pages Usenet messages	Ruby Ridge, Waco most reported in 335 messages (Table 10)
Mobilization for Action (Major Point 4)	Yes	Militia Web pages and Usenet messages	Internet preferred in a total of 148 messages (Table 11)

Variable	Measured?	How Measured?	Comment or Results
Social Control (Major Point 5)	Yes	Number of messages posted to Web archive	Control matters but not as specified by literature (Tables 12-13)
Orientation (Variable not part of Smelser's theory)	Yes	Militia Web pages, Usenet messages	Constitutionalist messages outnumber C.I. by 30% (Table 14)

5 A SERVICE EXAMPLE: A LOCAL ANTI-SMOKING PROGRAM FOR CHILDREN

Tobacco use is the number one cause of preventable deaths in the United States. Tobacco smoking annually kills 440,000 Americans. Ninety percent of adult smokers began smoking as teenagers, with 25 percent beginning as young as 12 years old. The average age for one to begin smoking is 14.5 years.[224] People who do not smoke as teenagers are likely to never smoke.[225] These statistics show that it is important that anti-smoking intervention be used for teenagers and even preteens.

Most people who smoke, whether they are young or old, claim they strongly desire to quit smoking. However, less than seven percent are able to stay free of tobacco use for one year when trying to quit without assistance. Nicotine is highly addictive both physiologically and psychologically. People smoke compulsively despite serious physical, social and even economic consequences.[226] Group social support appears to be fundamental in quitting smoking or in the decision not to smoke.

Most tobacco use begins with peer use of tobacco. Overall, peer use is more influential than parent use. The potential smoker comes to believe that many of their peers smoke, and this is a crucial factor in their subsequent decision to smoke.[227] A study of adult smokers who began to smoke as teenagers concluded that peer smoking and attitudes toward cigarettes have the strongest relationship to one's eventual involvement with cigarettes.[228]

Peer use of tobacco, though very important, is not the only source of pressure upon young people to smoke. Psychologists and social psychologists point out the potential influences of gender, home life, and mass media in the decision of young people to begin smoking. For example, smoking rates among school aged girls rose in the 1990s, and there is some evidence that young girls may start smoking earlier than young boys.[229] Girls that remain smoke free report being more ambivalent about their decision than are boys.[230] Issues of weight loss or weight control could be factors in a subsequent decision to take up smoking.[231] Further, depression in teen girls may lead to smoking, and data suggests the causal arrow could point both ways in this instance: smoking may increase the risk of depression and other depressive disorders.[232]

Parental and home influences can play an important role as well in the subsequent decision of children to smoke or not to smoke. Parents or relatives can be a help or a hindrance, depending upon what they do. On the negative side, instability in the home may be a strike against the youngster. Parental separation increases the likelihood that adolescents will start smoking.[233] If the split is permanent, the situation could be more serious. Adolescents who are raised in a home where one parent is absent are significantly more likely to smoke and to use alcohol.[234] One study found that having a live in father who smokes is a significant predictor of ninth graders who will eventually smoke.[235] Twin studies have gone so far as to suggest that youngsters could "inherit" smoking from their parents, with significant genetic contributions to initiation, age of onset, amount smoked and likelihood of quitting.[236] Nor should parents be considered the only influence in or near the home. The smoking habits of relatives, especially siblings, influence tobacco use by adolescents.[237]

In contrast, parental monitoring and help with school has been negatively associated with substance abuse, including smoking.[238] The authoritativeness of parenting was associated with lower levels of tobacco use; also, adolescents were particularly unlikely to use tobacco products when they both received authoritative parenting at home and were members of non-tobacco using peer groups.[239] One study reported that school aged children valued their parents' opinions, and wanted parents and other adults to take a clear stand against tobacco.[240]

Young people can be influenced by smoking imagery found in print media, particularly cigarette advertising that is targeted to their age group. A study in Arizona and Washington examined responses to cigarette advertisements among 400 adolescents, ages 12-17, who were surveyed in shopping malls.[241] The adolescents were presented with two ads for each of five youth brands (Marlboro, Newport, Camel, Kool, and Winston) and one ad for an adult brand (Merit), and were asked how often they had seen the ad, how much they liked the ad, and whether the ad made smoking more appealing. A substantial proportion of adolescents, especially smokers, liked the ads for the youth brands and believed the ads made smoking more appealing. The ads for Marlboro and the new Camel and Winston ads were especially attractive to adolescents.

A more subtle media influence upon young people is the pro-smoking imagery that appears in youth-oriented magazines that is not cigarette advertising per se. A qualitative study by MacFadyen, Amos, Hastings, and Parkes allowed British first-year students to give their impressions of the pro-smoking images found in such magazines and explored the relationship between this and their own smoking images and identities. The research found that: (1) this imagery was perceived to be, on the whole, attractive, sociable, and reassuring; (2) it supported young people's perceptions of smoking and reinforced their smoker identities; and (3) it has the potential to be more powerful than advertising imagery.[242]

Pro-smoking imagery in films can be another potent type of media exposure to smoking, and one study showed the negative influence that this kind of imagery can have upon young people.[243] The study found that, consistent with younger adolescents, older teens presented a predominantly nonchalant response to smoking imagery in film, which is a powerful indicator of the pervasiveness and acceptability of smoking in general.

Given these independent or conjoint influences upon young people, how is it possible that anti-smoking initiatives that target school-aged youngsters are effective? Hatcher and Scarpa held that some tobacco prevention plans do work. They argued persuasively that multi-component school based programs were some of the best programs. These efforts reduced tobacco use among peers, and assisted youngsters with learning how to cope with peer pressure, improving self esteem, developing communication skills and personal relationships, and managing anxiety. Misperceptions about the consequences of tobacco use were also discussed. The programs were delivered at school through group discussions, games, role-playing exercises, videos, and student worksheets.[244]

Gardner, Green and Marcus similarly discussed how peer groups could be used in a positive way as a means to reduce tobacco and other drug use. They suggested that positive peer groups that encourage alternative activities (that is, an alternative to alcohol, tobacco or drug use), supported healthy lifestyle choices, and allowed life skill practice would reduce substance abuse. An example they provided was the Gateway Project of Richmond, California that targets primary school aged youth. The students in the program participate in an after-school program two days each week. This gives the children an opportunity to bond with a group of peers in a positive, safe, and drug-free setting. The youths engage in recreational activities that emphasize the importance of basic living skills such as building self-esteem, making good decisions, and resisting peer pressure.[245]

The current report is concerned with evaluating Teens Offering Positive Supports (TOPS), a Big Brothers/Big Sisters Program. Big Brothers/Big Sisters is a national organization in which adult volunteers serve as mentors and role models to their Little Brother or Little Sister. Emphasis is placed on producing positive changes in the child, including a strengthened sense of self worth and improved relationships and performance at home, school, and in the community. TOPS is a special program of Big Brothers/Big Sisters in Southwest Louisiana. This is a school based mentoring program with various components informed in part by the literature on child and teen smoking. The program matched high school mentors with elementary school children believed to be at a high risk for smoking as well as alcohol and drug abuse. Fourth and fifth graders were selected for the program by their teachers and counselors because of specific social and academic needs. The teens met the younger students in a group setting one hour per week at their school, either during regular school hours or after school. A Big Brothers/Big Sisters staff member also attended. Together, they worked on academics, played games and participated in activities. They also discussed making the right choices, including abstinence from cigarettes, alcohol, and street drugs. A typical day in the program consisted of bigs helping littles with homework assignments, followed by teacher presentations on social skills, listening skills, or anger management, with corresponding exercises that bigs and littles worked on together. Anti-drug and anti-smoking segments were also presented, along with corresponding exercises that bigs and littles worked on together, such as role playing and student worksheets. Occasionally, an outside speaker would be invited to give a talk on topics relating to abstinence from drugs and alcohol. An underlying assumption, based on the peer-use research, was that kids working with kids – even if these were older peers working with much younger students - would be a more effective intervention than simply having adults warn the children about the dangers of drugs, violence, and smoking. For the most part, these older peers were raised in the same communities as the younger students, and as such have had some common experiences – including dealing with the pressures and stresses that may lead the younger students to smoke someday.

The specific purpose of this research was to assess the effectiveness of this approach as it was adopted by Southwest Louisiana school districts in conjunction with Big Brothers/Big Sisters. The program allowed for some local variation or flexibility in terms of how the program was carried out. This allowed us as researchers to determine if certain variations of the program may be better than others, or more effective in reaching the goals of the program. For example, at one school an innovative new pilot program called the "Island Project" was launched as part of the TOPS program. The research evaluated the effectiveness of this new program and compared its effectiveness to more traditional ways of carrying out the TOPS program.

Method

The subjects in the study were 194 "big" brothers and sisters along with their designated "little" brother or sister in the TOPS Program during the 2002-2003 school year. There were 110 "littles" who attended various elementary schools in southwest Louisiana, while the 84 "bigs" were juniors and seniors in various high schools in the same geographic region. The littles group consisted of 42.7 percent males and 57.3 percent females. There were 31.8 percent of the littles that considered themselves nonwhite and 68.2 percent that claimed to be white. The bigs were composed of 29.8 percent males and 70.2 percent females. The bigs were mostly white, 90.5 percent, while only 9.5 percent were nonwhite.

The subjects were divided into three groups. One group was a control group that attended school along with the TOPS students but did not participate at all in TOPS or in the Big Brothers/Big Sisters program. The second group is an experimental group which offered the usual TOPS program with components dealing with the importance of abstaining from cigarettes, alcohol, and other drugs. The third group was an experimental group that engaged in the special yearlong activity called the Island Project. In this project, each big/little pair was asked to create their own Island or country as a team activity. There were 10 sessions available to complete this project. The big/little pairs named their island, created an exchange rate, created a government, constructed a physical model of their island, and various other tasks. In both of the experimental groups, the littles met with their mentors or bigs at the school during regular school hours; and, a TOPS Big Brother/Big Sister Coordinator met with the group to plan and supervise their activities.

All groups were given a pre-test at the beginning of the program (soon after school began in the fall) and a post test in the spring. The tests included background questions about race, age, and sex, as well as questions concerning their attitude toward the use of alcohol, tobacco, and street drugs. An important series of questions asked about their peers and their use or abuse of alcohol, tobacco or street drugs. Additionally, there was scalar measuring of impulsivity, self-esteem and self-concept. Improvement in these areas was expected as an outcome of the program in addition to reduced cigarette and drug use. Teachers and bigs also completed questionnaires about any behavioral changes that they may have observed in the little brothers or sisters. These are standard questionnaires utilized by Big Brothers/Big Sisters to evaluate the quality of the big-little match.

Variables and Measurement

The questionnaire administered to teachers and to the "bigs" who mentored the elementary students consisted of 23 items. Questions 1-21 asked the teachers or mentors to rate how much change they have observed in the "littles" during the course of the TOPS program: "Much Better," "A Little Better," "No Change," "A Little Worse," or "Much Worse." Scores were assigned on a Likert scale with five points assigned to an evaluation of "Much Better" and one point to an evaluation of "Much Worse." If appropriate, the teacher or mentor could say that they "Don't Know" how much of a change has been made, or the characteristic being observed is "Not a Problem" for that particular student. The specific questions asked for the teachers or mentors to rate the changes in the littles along three dimensions, Confidence (questions 1-6), Competence (questions 7-16) and Caring (questions 17-21). The final questions of the instrument asked if there had been any improvement in the student's grades in any school subject since the beginning of the school year, and if so, in how many subjects.

The questionnaire administered to the little brothers and sisters consisted of a few preliminary demographic questions followed by 60 more questions. Questions 1-59 asked the subjects if they agree or disagree with statements such as "I am friendly," "I am popular," "I like to dare kids to do things," "It is harmful if children use street drugs," and "My friends use tobacco." For each question of this type, the student was asked to respond to the statement by designating one of the following: Never (Strongly Disagree), Rarely (Disagree), Sometimes, Mostly (Agree), and Always (Strongly Agree). Responses were scored on a Likert scale with Never equaling 1 and Always equaling 5. Individual questions contributed to various scales that measured concepts central to the purposes of the research. Question 60 was about the student's home life. It asked if the student's parents are married, live together unmarried, separated, divorced, or deceased. Questions that contributed to scale measurement are noted below.

Self Concept Scale: Questions 1-22, adapted from Fischer and Corcoran, and Lipsitt.[246]

Impulsivity Scale: Questions 23-40, adapted from Fischer and Corcoran, and Hirschfield.[247]

Parental Nurturance Scale: Questions 41 and 42, adapted from Fischer and Corcoran, and Buri.[248]

Self Esteem Scale: Questions 43-45, adapted from Fischer and Corcoran, and Rosenberg.[249]

Perception of Harm to Adults and Children From Using Alcohol, Tobacco and Street Drugs: Questions 46 through 51. Subscales measured the student's perception of the harm produced by alcohol, tobacco, street drugs, or all of them together in combination as used by children, by adults, or by both.

Deviancy: Questions 52 and 55.

Peer Use of Alcohol and Tobacco: Questions 53 and 54. Question 53: "My friends use alcohol." Question 54: "My friends use tobacco."

Locus of Control (External or Internal): Questions 56 through 59.

For each scale, there was a comparison of the students' pre test scores with the post test scores. In some scales it was expected that the post test scores would be lower, for example, the score for Peer Use of Alcohol and Tobacco. For other scales, such as the Self Concept Scale, it was expected that the higher scores would be on the post test rather than on the pre test.

Results

Teachers' evaluation data appears in Table 15. The teachers of the littles reported that in 80 percent of the littles there was some improvement in their grades since the beginning of school, and in the average case there was improvement in two academic subjects. Behaviorally, there was substantial improvement noted along multiple factors since the beginning of the school year: self-confidence; ability to express feelings; interest in hobbies; personal hygiene; sense of the future; use of community resources; use of school resources; class participation; ability to avoid substance abuse; ability to avoid early parenting; trust toward teacher; respect for other cultures; relationships with family; relationships with peers; and relationships with other adults. The mentors or bigs agreed with all but one of the teachers' improvement ratings and noted improvements in five additional areas. These included: ability to make decisions; academic performance; attitude toward school; school preparedness; and ability to avoid delinquency.

Among the littles, the two experimental groups were compared to the control group using a comparison of means along some key variables in Table 16. The mean self concept scores declined in both

Table 15. Teachers' Evaluation of the TOPS Program*

Trait	N	Mean	SD	Improvement
Self-Confidence	42	4.0476	.8250	1.05
Able to express feelings	42	4.0000	.7651	1.00
Has interests or hobbies	30	4.1333	.7303	1.13
Personal hygiene	30	3.9333	.7849	0.93
Sense of the future	36	4.1111	.6667	1.11
Uses community resources	28	4.0357	.7445	1.03
Uses school resources	39	4.0256	.6684	1.02
Class participation	40	3.9250	.8286	0.92
Able to avoid substance abuse	12	4.4167	.9962	1.41
Able to avoid early parenting	11	4.6364	.6742	1.63
Shows trust toward you	39	4.2308	.7767	1.23
Respects other cultures	35	4.2000	.6325	1.20
Relationship with family	33	4.2424	.6139	1.24
Relationship with peers	39	4.0256	.8425	1.02
Rel. w/other adults	38	4.2105	.7036	1.21

*For each item, teachers could elect to say that they "didn't know" if there had been improvement, or that the trait being measured was "not a problem" for that student.

---

of the experimental groups, more so in the special Island Project than in the Other Experimental Group, which was the more traditional way of delivering the TOPS program. Mean peer use of alcohol and tobacco declined in the experimental groups, although the decline was less in the Island Project than in the Other Experimental Group. Mean impulsive behavior scores rose, and the scores were higher in the Island Project than in the Other Experimental Group. The mean perceived harm posed by alcohol to children was lowest in the Island Project when comparing means across all three groups.

Table 16. Means and Standard Deviations for Selected Variables, by Experimental or Control Group

Group	Self Concept	Peer Use of Alcohol and Tobacco	Impulsivity	Perceived Harm, Alcohol, Tobacco and Street Drug Use for Children
Island Project Mean N Standard Dev.	 -3.1905 21 12.1310	 -.2632 19 2.8644	 5.4500 20 12.3735	 -.7368 19 4.9536

Table 16 Continued				
Group	**Self Concept**	**Peer Use of Alcohol and Tobacco**	**Impulsivity**	**Perceived Harm, Alcohol, Tobacco and Street Drug Use for Children**
Other Experimental Mean N Standard Dev.	 -1.1279 86 12.0614	 -.5169 89 2.7141	 4.2247 89 12.7936	 .5056 89 3.2055
Control Mean N Standard Dev.	 .5882 17 13.1959	 1.6111 18 2.3298	 7.8889 18 11.1508	 -.6111 18 4.3944
Total Mean N Standard Dev.	 -1.2419 124 12.1751	 -.1746 126 2.7657	 4.9370 127 12.4828	 .1587 126 3.6995

Table 17. One-Way ANOVA Results Comparing Means Scores on Selected Variables, by Experimental and Control Groups

Variable	Sum of Squares	Df	Mean Square	F Sig.
Self Concept	BG + 137.793 WG 18094.949 T 18232.742	2 121 123	68.897 149.545	.461 .632
Peer Use of Tobacco and Alcohol	BG 67.972 WG 888.187 T 956.159	2 123 125	33.986 7.221	4.707 .011
Impulsivity	BG 207.263 WG 19426.233 T 19633.496	2 124 126	103.631 156.663	.661 .518
Perceived Harm, Alcohol Use for Children	BG 8.751 WG 179.694 T 188.444	2 123 125	4.375 1.461	2.995 .054

Table 17 Continued				
Variable	**Sum of Squares**	**Df**	**Mean Square**	**F Sig.**
Perceived Harm, Alcohol, Tobacco and Street Drug Use for Children	BG 36.616 WG 1674.209 T 1710.825	2 123 125	18.308 13.611	1.345 .264
Perceived Harm, Street Drug Use for Children	BG 3.257 WG 215.101 T 218.357	2 123 125	1.628 1.749	.931 .397
Perceived Harm, Alcohol Use for Children and Adults	BG 10.067 WG 707.211 T 717.278	2 123 125	5.033 5.750	.875 .419

+ BG = Between Groups; WG = Within Groups; T = Total

in the Island Project than in the Other Experimental Group. The mean perceived harm posed by alcohol to children was lowest in the Island Project when comparing means across all three groups.

The experimental groups were compared to the control group using One-Way ANOVA in Table 17. These results indicated that a benefit that accrued to individuals participating in the TOPS program was a reduced peer use of alcohol and tobacco (p=.011).

This was an expected outcome of the program, and to a certain extent validates the time and effort expended by littles, bigs, teachers, and Big Brothers/Big Sisters administrators as they participated in the program. At the same time, the following factors were not statistically significant when comparing the experimental and control groups: the perceived harm that could be done by children using alcohol ($p=.054$) and the perceived harm that could be done by children using a combination of alcohol, tobacco, and street drugs ($p=.264$). Gender comparisons of mean scores along the selected variables utilizing t-tests produced no statistically significant results. An ANOVA comparison of the means of selected variables according to parental status – that is, whether the student's parents are married, living together and not married, separated, divorced, or deceased – likewise produced no statistically significant results.

Discussion

The evaluation of the TOPS program was mixed. The program was praised by teachers and mentors, and the program did have the effect of reducing peer use of alcohol and tobacco among 110 grade school students in Southwest Louisiana. This is something that was a basic expectation of the program, and it is a "bottom line" kind of result that may, in itself, be an argument for the continuation of the program. However, program administrators had hoped for more positive results, and they might be wondering why, on many of the key variables, the program failed to show a significant difference in the mean scores in the experimental groups and the control group. A further analysis of those results by gender and by parental status of the participating students failed to shed any light on why the program was not more productive.

It was also found that the local variation on the basic program offered by TOPS called the "Island Project" produced idiosyncratic results. For example, students who participated in the Island project, which was conducted at only one school in Southwest Louisiana, reported a decrease in peer use of alcohol and tobacco, but also reported a lowering in the perception that alcohol is harmful to children. This is an unexpected negative result for which there is no concrete explanation at present. If anything, it was expected that the prolonged contact with a positive peer group would produce even more positive results than other interventions. This clearly did not happen, and the results signal a potential "red flag" that all innovative approaches may not immediately produce positive outcomes, and early monitoring of the new approaches is in order. If problems are discovered in such programs, corrective measures may be necessary to produce better results. In the worst case, the new program may have to be discontinued.

This unexpected result should also alert us to something pointed out about peer based programs by a recent reviewer of them.[250] The reviewer stated that peer influences on smoking are more subtle than commonly thought and need to be examined more carefully, including consideration of larger social contexts such as the family, neighborhoods, and the media. In the instance cited above, the Island Project, any number of local factors could have contributed to the poor results, including enigmatic characteristics of the school district, the individuals supervising the program, or the big brothers and sisters. Awareness that such local factors may influence research results might assist in interpreting equally anomalous outcomes in other studies. Such local influences were unmeasured in this study, as were the pervasive media influences that the literature review suggested could be an important influence in the youngster's decision to smoke.

This study also does not explore the specific dynamics of the decline in peer use. The results suggest that peers have quit smoking and drinking, but it was not known for sure if the students picked new nonsmoking peers, or if students' old, established peers quit smoking during the school year. What may be happening is a more general process in which the social desirability of smoking and drinking is being decreased by the students' participation in the program. More evaluation research of similar programs targeting grade school children is needed to further explore this social dynamic.

A bigger picture in which to evaluate the results would be to consider the long range benefits of this program. The research reported upon in this paper has been conducted in Southwest Louisiana since 2000, and each year since then the data has indicated significant declines in peer use of alcohol and tobacco. In selected years there has also been significant increases in the subjects' perception that drug use is harmful to children and adults; increases in mean self concept scores; decreased involvement in deviant behaviors such as skipping school and criminal activity, and declines in impulse behavior. Teachers and mentors participating in the program have consistently rated it very positively.[251] Moreover, each yearly cohort that participates in the program is a unique group, and the social dynamics of the peer groups and their supervisors thus may have variable qualities from year to year. This in turn may affect the precise nature of any behavioral improvements, or lack thereof noted in the TOPS students for that particular school year. The point here is that each year's results are different, and we would not expect the same results each year given that new cohorts are participating in the program.

Are the benefits that accrue from the program lasting? As the grade school children advance into middle and high school, do they continue to abstain from smoking and choose peers who do not smoke or drink? A follow up study of the littles that participated in TOPS in Southwest Louisiana since 2000 might provide some preliminary data. We recommend that, where possible, anti-smoking programs targeting grade school children include a longitudinal panel design that can track the participating students at regular intervals, and gather data about their smoking status and any situational factors that influence them to smoke or to abstain from smoking.

6 CONCLUSION: SURVIVING THE LOWER TIERS

My purpose in writing this book was to provide a time capsule of what it was like to be a sociologist in a lower ranked teaching institution, and to highlight what goes on in some of the lower tiered schools, not that these institutions are "representative" of other schools, but more for the purpose of providing one example (among many possibilities) of how sociology is accomplished in the lower ranked institutions. I believe that this purpose has been fulfilled, but along the way something unusual happened. I learned more about myself, my institution, and my place in the whole order of American sociology, a learning process that extended well beyond an initial observation that my life is at the bottom of the heap and that my viewpoint is "from below."

Sociology really is a caste system, as most of the stratification studies of sociology departments make clear. Val Burris' work is simply more recent evidence in support of that point.[252] During the period of self examination that I encountered in writing this book, I was even more aware of how brilliant was the advice that Caplow and McGee gave to serious, Master's-seeking sociology students long ago, when they wrote that the student's first choice of graduate school would have an everlasting mark upon his or her career.[253] In retrospect, I think that this advice was both far sighted and brilliant, and I now admit to some latent disappointment with the advice that my Master's level sociological theory teacher gave me when I was a Master's student: that theoretically, anyone can end up at Harvard by producing exemplary research and writing skills.[254] That advice was obviously false and it was just plain wrong to give it without having the facts in hand. Today, the first choice of a graduate school appears to be more important than it ever has been, as it is an entry into a specific caste from which there is almost nothing in the way of social mobility. The decision amounts to choosing a tier level from which there is probably no escape, no matter how brilliant the student perceives themselves to be or how hard they work at advancing in their career.

Moreover, the nature of the caste system of sociology also sheds light upon how important it is for young sociology majors in undergraduate school to do well their first year – of undergraduate school. I have advised many otherwise bright youngsters who would have had a shot at the Ivy League as sociology graduate students were it not for some hard partying and a bad start freshman year, a start that is nearly impossible to overcome later in terms of overall GPA.

I learned and appreciated the skills of my colleagues and was proud to be a part of the "fictive kin" arrangement where we all need each other in order to navigate through the scarce resources.[255]

I learned about how myopic life can be at the bottom of sociology and how trying to generalize my experiences to other schools can be futile. I can also appreciate now that there is great diversity in Tier 4, perhaps more than I'll ever know given my tendency to be trapped in a library and not networking as much as I should be with others in my own Tier and in other tiers.

I can testify that life is or can be mostly satisfying in Tier 4 if you like the town you live in and can tolerate your boss and colleagues (and they can tolerate you – no small task at times). If this is the case, there is at least a potential for a modicum of satisfaction with work and with life. I have now spent enough time in Tier 4 that I can recommend some ways in which the whole situation can be made livable if this state of affairs has not yet been achieved.

Travel. This travel might be simply recreational or regenerative, that is to recharge batteries and to make good use of any cultural advantages that might apply to your region of residence. But it could also be to gain perspectives and experiences that might later be used to enrich teaching and research. Sometimes it is a good thing in itself if used simply to relax – people need a reasonable amount of time off, and it seems that the longer you've worked the job, the more you need. Some have managed to create a daily schedule that allows for at least some enjoyment of the finer things in life (or the small pleasures as circumstances may dictate). This allows you to figuratively "travel" without going too far away from home. Stress management counselors often suggest this as a way of dealing with the stresses of life.

A second job. A skill that can be parlayed into a second income is useful, perhaps even a requirement at the lowest paying institutions. For example, a friend of mine at another school is a Ph.D. sociologist and also an M.S.W. A private counseling practice augments his low salary as a sociology professor. Some of the most satisfied professors at the school I work at are those who parlayed the second job into what amounts to a first job, at least in terms of income earned. That is, the teaching became like a second job where minimal input was required compared with the 'other" job that had acquired a first priority. However, this appeared to apply most to the older, after-tenure types who had settled in at the institution as opposed to younger faculty. Younger people, the restless types, spent a good deal of time trying to bail out (move on to "greener pastures") once they got the essence of daily life at the school. And for those younger ones who tried to stay and to do too much – to settle in at the institution and work a demanding second job - the results can be disastrous. A talented, young, untenured faculty member who tried to teach full time at a sociology teaching institution and also work full time as a researcher for a major corporation was sent packing after two years.[256]

Networking. Keeping alive a network of friends and colleagues can help out with the publication requirement, especially as it relates to journals seeking specialty papers or ones that the larger and more selective mainstream (upper class) journals might not touch. Sharing skills and data with colleagues can only help in this regard. Keep in touch with those who leave, as they may be the source of a new job - a way out of your current predicament if you simply hate it. If nothing else, their experiences bring a fresh perspective and a way to compare your own experiences on the bottom with someone else.

Family. Spending time with your family is a stabilizing influence. Get to know them once again, and explore your spiritual side if that is something that is important to you.

Awards. Seek out all that apply to you and you have a reasonable chance of winning. Winning one can be terrifically self validating. The trick here might be not to tire out oneself needlessly by applying for every single award or fellowship that comes your way, but to be selective, and to go after the ones that are achievable. It is probably more important to spend time writing journal articles or books than it is to spend time chasing large research contracts. Consider your competition when applying for these awards. Are you really going to wrestle that award away from Harvard and become a local hero? Probably not. After awhile, by trial and error more than anything else, you get an idea of the kinds of awards or fellowships that are reasonably within your grasp or within your skill as a grant writer; let the other opportunities go as they may drain your creative strength. The process of applying for such awards and grants can be exhausting. Use summertime for enrichment. And why not pursue more education? I came across an opportunity during 2005 when a major insurance carrier was offering scholarships to full time college teaching faculty as an opportunity for continuing education and academic enrichment. I applied, as the process was not time consuming and the potential rewards were great.

Moving up. There is always the struggle immediately ahead: to get promoted beyond your current job. Find out what you need to do and make this kind of professional activity a priority. Work hard at it, as it has its own rewards, financial and in terms of prestige. Even at the full professor rank, thoughts of a future designation of Professor Emeritus may provide some incentive to work hard, if that designation is something that is important or meaningful to you.

Perks. There may not be many in the lower tiers; but seek out any that are there and relish them.

Specialization. Specialization comes easy to college professors as it was a requirement for their doctorate. But why not go beyond that? If you enjoy research and can build something even greater out of your dissertation research, why not give it a try?

Opportunism. Consider speaking engagements or presentations at professional meetings as opportunities to pursue even more specialized kinds of research. In 2002, I was invited to conduct a seminar on death and dying for a group of home health workers. Intrigued that the information presented might be somewhat unique, I performed a literature review, only to discover that little had been written on the subject. I kept the notes from the presentation, wrote them up in article form, and submitted them to a journal.

Professional associations. Join as many professional associations as you can afford to join. Then, volunteer to do some thankless task. This willingness to work may be your bridge to a more important task. Many times, the people who ended up as presidents of sociological associations have a story that runs something like this: "my first assignment was when I volunteered to count votes for president at the 1980 meetings; and amazingly enough, this plugged me in to the hierarchy of the association, and they kept giving me more to do."[257]

Extra income. Time and energy permitting, pursue overload teaching opportunities such as continuing education classes and "between term" classes, as these allow extra income and the possibility of widening out your academic interests and making you more valuable to your department.

Technology. Give technology a try in you haven't already done so. Not that you'll become a computer geek; but you might start to think more like one, and might not be afraid to give some technological gadgets a try in your classroom. Students appear to enjoy this, and will appreciate it if you give it a try. Some know computers well enough that they can help you out if your presentation will not run.

Change equals opportunity. View change as an opportunity for advancement. Many who have worked full time at sociological research centers and enjoyed a long run of continuing contracts know full well that the end of the road can come fairly soon when projects are not renewed, or the possibility of riding another wave of grants is impossible. View such situations as opportunities for change that could be good for you. Even not making tenure at your school could be such a blessing in disguise. Occasionally there are stories of people let go at a low ranking school, only to catch on with a higher ranked school and those people go on to a rich and fulfilling career.[258]

Stay healthy. Work on your health. If you truly enjoy the security of your job and are generally satisfied with it, one way to increase your longevity at the school is to work on your health. This is especially true at schools that do not mind an "old" faculty and will not immediately try to chase you out the door once you've reached a given age.

Stay positive. If at all possible, accentuate the positive. Teaching in the bottom tiers, if done well, can be a very secure kind of life. True, there are no bright marquee lights in Tier 4, and at times the structural problems such as the budget woes can seem overwhelming. Administrative problems and the personalities of some colleagues can be maximally irritating. But employment is mostly secure, and that is a strong positive point to focus on.

This book has been a look at life in the lower tiered sociology teaching institutions. There is both joy and pain here along with a good deal of frustration. However, life is tolerable and even satisfying to a certain degree. For doctoral candidates at the lower ranked schools, this book could be a glimpse into their immediate futures if college teaching is in their plans. I submit that the structural conditions of sociology are such that the rules of the game are not going to change anytime soon. While the upper tier controls the resources and prestige of the discipline, much of the heavy lifting and the spirit of the discipline reside in the lower ranked schools. This will be forever so, for as Robert Merton once observed: "For unto every one that hath shall be given, and he shall have abundance: but from him that hath not shall be taken away even that which he hath.[259]

ABOUT THE AUTHOR

Stan C. Weeber (Ph.D, University of North Texas, 2000) is an Associate Professor of Sociology and Criminal Justice at McNeese State University in Lake Charles, Louisiana. His interests in sociology include storytelling sociology, political sociology, social movements, and sociological theory. The author or editor of 18 books, his work has appeared in *The American Sociologist*, *The Sociological Quarterly*, the *Journal of Public Management and Social Policy*, *Journal of Sociology, Social Work and Social Welfare*, *International Review of Modern Sociology*, the *Canadian Review of Sociology and Anthropology*, the *Contemporary Law and Justice Journal*, the *Journal of Popular Culture*, the *Journal of Law, Politics, and Societies*, the *Journal of Global Analysis*, and several other journals. In addition, Dr. Weeber serves on the editorial boards of four international sociology journals. In 2010, he participated in the Oxford Roundtable on Social Justice, a social issues think tank at Oxford University.

NOTES

[1] Randal Collins, "The Organizational Politics of the ASA," *The American Sociologist*, 21, 4, Winter, 1990: 311-315; Howard S. Becker, "The Most Critical Issue Facing the ASA," *The American Sociologist*, 21, 4, Winter, 1990: 321-323; Peter Rossi, "The Future of Sociology," *Contemporary Sociology*, 19, 4, July, 1990: 623-624; Stephen Turner, "Symposium: The Future of Sociological Theory," *The American Sociologist*, 21, 3, Fall, 1990: 275-299; Anthony Orum, "Symposium: Ethical Issues in Scholarly Publication," *The American Sociologist*, 21,1, Spring, 1990: 67-95; Stephen Turner and Jonathan Turner, *The Impossible Science: An Institutional Analysis of American Sociology*. Newbury Park, CA: Sage Publications, Inc., 1990; Bonnie Berry, "An Account of a Professional Ethics Violation in Sociology," *The American Sociologist*, 22, 3-4, Fall-Winter, 1991: 261-266; "Symptoms of Administrative Threats to Abolish Sociology: A Panel for Chairpersons," panel presented at the annual meetings of the Southern Sociological Society, 1991; David Fabianic, "Declining Enrollments of Sociology Majors: Department Responses," *The American Sociologist*, 22, 1, Spring, 1991: 25-36; Alan Wolfe, "Weak Sociology/Strong Sociologists: Consequences and Contradictions of a Field in Turmoil," *Social Research*, 59, 4, Winter, 1992: 759-779; John Galliher, "The Three Eras of the American Sociologist," *The American Sociologist*, 23, 2, Summer, 1992; Howard Becker and William Rau, "Sociology in the 1990s," *Society*, 30, 1, November-December, 1992: 70-74; Peter Berger, "Sociology, A Disinvitation?" *Society*, 30, 1, November-December, 1992: 12-18; Terence Halliday and Morris Janowitz (Eds). *Sociology and Its Publics: The Forms and Fates of Disciplinary Organization*. Chicago: University of Chicago

Press, 1992; Dan Krier and William G. Staples, "Seen But Unseen: Part-Time Faculty and Institutional Surveillance and Control," *The American Sociologist*, 24, 3-4, Fall-Winter, 1993: 119-134; Ted Vaughn, Gideon Sjoberg and Larry Reynolds (Eds.) *A Critique of Contemporary American Sociology*. Dix Hills, NY: General Hall, 1993; Irving L. Horowitz, *The Decomposition of Sociology*. New York: Oxford University Press, 1993; American Sociological Association, *Report on the Discipline*. Washington, D.C.: American Sociological Association, 1993; Anthony Haynor and Joseph Varacalli, "Sociology's Fall From Grace: The Six Deadly Sins of a Discipline at the Crossroads," *Quarterly Journal of Ideology*, 16, 1-2, June, 1993: 3-29; American Sociological Association, *Report on the Discipline*. Washington, D.C.: American Sociological Association, 1994; Nancy Herman and Larry T. Reynolds, *Symbolic Interaction: An Introduction to Social Psychology*. Dix Hills, NY: General Hall, 1994; Gregory Weiss and Dretha Phillips, "Participation of Sociologists at Two-Year and Four-Year Colleges in the American Sociological Association," *The American Sociologist*, 25, 3, Fall, 1994: 37-52; Rick Ponting, "Sociology: A Discipline in Jeopardy?" *Society*, 19, 2, May, 1995: 9-11; Charles Cappell, "An Empirical Comment on the State of Sociology," *The American Sociologist*, 26, 2, Summer, 1995: 78-123; Norval Glenn, "A Critique of Twenty Family and Marriage and the Family Textbooks," *Family Relations*, 46, 3, July, 1997: 197-208; Walter Gove and Nancy Malcom, "Can Sociology Be A Science?:The Issue of Gender and Sex-Dimorphic Characteristics," *The American Sociologist*, 28, 4, Winter, 1997: 9-30; Barry Johnston, "The Contemporary Crisis and the Social Relations Department at Harvard: A Case Study in Hegemony and Disintegration," *The American Sociologist*, 29, 3, Fall, 1998: 26-42; William F. Whyte, "Rethinking Sociology: Applied and Basic Research," *The American Sociologist*, 29, 1, Spring, 1998: 16-19; Larry Reynolds, "Two Deadly Diseases and One Nearly Fatal Cure," *The American Sociologist*, 29, 1, Spring, 1998: 20-37; Carl Hand and Bennett Judkins, "Disciplinary Schisms: Subspecialty 'Drift' and the Fragmentation of Sociology," *The American Sociologist*, 30, 1, Spring, 1999: 18-36; John Goldthorpe, "Causation, Statistics, and Sociology," *European Sociological Review*, 17, 1, March, 2000: 1-20; B. Keith, " Taking Stock of the Discipline: Some Reflections on the State of American Sociology," *The American Sociologist* 31, 1, 2000: 5-14; Jonathan B. Imber, "Public Sociology: From Social Facts to Literary Act," *Social Forces*, 80, 1, September, 2001: 26-42; Stephen Cole, *What's Wrong With Sociology?* New Brunswick, NJ: Transaction, 2001; Joel Best, "Giving It Away: The Ironies of Sociology's Place in Academia," *The American Sociologist*, 32, 1, Spring, 2001: 107-113; Myles Kelleher, "The Professional Ideology of Social Pathologists Transformed: The New Political Orthodoxy in Sociology," *The American Sociologist*, 32, 3, Winter, 2001: 70-88; Mitchell Miller, Richard Wright and David Daniels, "Is Deviance 'Dead'? The Decline of a Sociological Research Specialization," *The American Sociologist*, 32, 3, Fall, 2001: 43-59; Lawrence Nichols, "Editor's Introduction: Sociology and Its Specialty Fields," *The American Sociologist*, 32, 3, Summer, 2001: 3-4; Orlando Patterson, "The Last Sociologist,"

New York Times, May 19, 2002; Joel Best, "Killing the Messenger: The Social Problems of Sociology," *Social Problems*, 50, 1, February, 2003: 1-13.

[2] Robert Lynd, *Knowledge for What? The Place of Social Science in American Culture*. Princton, NJ: Princeton University Press, 1939; Pitirim Sorokin, *Fads and Foibles in Modern Sociology and Related Sciences*. Chicago: Regnery Company, 1956; Pitirim Sorokin and Walter Lunden, *Power and Morality: Who Shall Guard the Guardians*? Boston: P. Sargent, 1959; C. Wright Mills, *The Sociological Imagination*. New York: Oxford University Press, 1959; Alvin Gouldner, *The Coming Crisis of Western Sociology*. New York: Basic Books, 1970; Randall Collins, "Is 1980s Sociology in the Doldrums?" *American Journal of Sociology*, 91, 6, May, 1986: 1336-1355; Jennifer Turpin, Michael Webber, Anne Roschelle, William Edwards, and Joseph Angilella, "Surviving and Thriving: Bringing Back Sociology at the University of San Francisco," *The American Sociologist*, 27, 3, Fall, 1996: 8-26; Oliver Cox, *Capitalism and American Leadership*. New York: Philosophical Library, 1962; Maurice Stein and Arthur Vidich, *Sociology on Trial*. Englewood Cliffs, NJ: Prentice Hall, 1963; Irving L. Horowitz, "The Life and Death of Project Camelot," *Trans-Action*, 3, 1, November-December, 1965: 44-47; Irving L. Horowitz, "Social Science Yogis and Military Commissars," *Trans-Action*, 5, 6, May, 1968: 29-38; Lewis Coser, "Two Methods in Search of a Substance," *American Sociological Review*, 40, 6, December, 1975: 691-700; Alfred Lee, "Sociology for Whom?" *American Sociological Review*, 41, 6, December, 1976: 925-936; Allen Liska, "The Dissipation of Sociological Social Psychology," *The American Sociologist*, 12, 1, February, 1977: 2-8; Reece McGee, "The College Market in Commercial Publishing: The Case of the Convertible?" *The American Sociologist*, 12, 3, August, 1977: 102-107; Lee Ellis, "The Decline and Fall of Sociology, 1975-2000," *The American Sociologist*, 12, 2, May, 1977: 56-66; Howard Tuckman, Jaime Caldwell and William Vogler, "Part Timers and the Academic Labor Market of the Eighties," *The American Sociologist*, 13, 4, November, 1978: 184-195; David Gray, "American Sociology: Plight and Promise," *The American Sociologist*, 14, 1, February, 1979: 35-42; Allen Grimshaw, "What Ought Sociology to be Doing? And Why Aren't We Doing It?" *The American Sociologist*, 14, 2, May, 1979: 68-69; Jessie Bernard, *The Female World*. New York: Free Press, 1981; Amos Hawley, "Whither the ASA?" *The American Sociologist*, 16, 2, May, 1981: 108-110; Alfred Lee, "How Can the American Sociological Association Become More Useful?" *The American Sociologist*, 16, 2, May, 1981: 93-97; David Watts, Alvin Short and Clarence Schultz, "Applied Sociology and the Current Crisis," *Teaching Sociology*, 11, 1, October, 1983: 47-61; Mark Wardell and Stephen Turner (Eds.) *Sociological Theory in Transition*. Boston: Allen Unwin, 1986; Stephen Turner, "Underdetermination and the Promise of Statistical Sociology," *Sociological Theory*, 5, 2, Fall, 1987: 172-184; Dusky Lee Smith and Larry T. Reynolds, "The Sociologist as Critical Apologist: William Graham Sumner as an Anti-Imperialist," *Humanity and Society*, 11, 1, February, 1987: 58-79; Richard Berstein, "Metaphysical Critique and Utopia," *The Review of Metaphysics*, 42, 2,

December, 1988: 255-273; Herbert Danzger, "Undergraduate Education in Sociology as Career Training: The Case for an Internship Program," *Teaching Sociology*, 16, 1, January, 1988: 41-48; Peter Berger, "Whose Keeper? Social Science and Moral Obligation," *New York Times Book Review*, 94, 43, October 22, 1989: 34; Ben Agger, "Do Books Write Authors? A Study of Disciplinary Hegemony," *Teaching Sociology*, 17, 3, July, 1989: 365-369; Elizabeth Higginbotham, "It's Time to Talk About Privilege: Developing an Inclusive Curriculum in Sociology," paper read at the annual meetings of the American Sociological Association, 1989; Jonathan Turner, "The Disintegration of American Sociology: Pacific Sociological Association 1988 Presidential Address," *Sociological Perspectives*, 32, 4, Winter, 1989: 419-433.

[3] Turpin *et. al*: 9.

[4] *Ibid.*

[5] Raymond Hughes, A *Study of Graduate Schools of America*. Oxford, OH: Miami University, 1925; Raymond Hughes, *A Study of Graduate Schools of America.* Oxford, OH: Miami University, 1934; Hayward Keniston, *Graduate Study and Research in the Arts and Sciences at the University of Pennsylvania.* Philadelphia: University of Pennsylvania Press, 1959; Allen Carrter, *An Assessment of Quality in Graduate Education*. Washington, D.C.: American Council on Education, 1970; Lyle Jones, Gardner Lindsay and Porter Coggeshall, *An Assessment of Research-Doctorate Programs in the United States – Social and Behavioral Sciences.* Washington, D.C.: National Academy Press, 1982; Marvin Goldberger, Brendan Maher and Pamela Flattau, Research-Doctorate Programs in the United States: Continuity and Change. Washington, D.C.: National Academy Press, 1995.

[6] Jeffrey Alexander, *Twenty Lectures: Sociological Theory Since World War II.* New York: Columbia University Press, 1987.

[7] Stephanie Baldi, "Departmental Quality Ratings and Visibility: The Advantages of Size and Age," *The American Sociologist*, 28, 1, Spring, 1997: 89-101; David Webster, Clifton Conrad and Eric Jensen, "Objective and Reputational Rankings of Ph.D.-Granting Departments of Sociology, 1965-1982," *Sociological Focus*, 21, 2, April, 1988: 177-198.

[8] Stephanie Baldi, "Changes in the Stratification Structure of Sociology, 1964-1992," *The American Sociologist*, 25, 4, Winter, 1994: 28-43.

[9] *Ibid.*

[10] Val Burris, "The Academic Caste System: Prestige Hierarchies in Ph.D. Exchange Networks," *American Sociological Review*, 69, 2, April, 2004: 239-264.

[11] Theodore Caplow and Reece McGee, *The Academic Marketplace*. New York: Basic Books, 1958.

[12] *U.S. News and World Report*, Rankings of Doctoral Granting Institutions, 2004.

[13] Burris, *ibid.*

[14] Patterson, *ibid.*

[15] Lowell Hargens, "Sociologists' Assessment of the State of Sociology, 1969-1984," *The American Sociologist*, 21, 2, Fall, 1990: 200-208.

[16] Harriet Zuckerman and Robert Merton, "Patterns of Evaluation in Science: Institutionalization, Structure and Function of the Referee System," *Minerva*, 9, 1, 1971: 66-100.

[17] *The American Sociologist*, 32, 3, Fall, 2001: 60-72.

[18] Talcott Parsons, "Some Problems Confronting Sociology as a Profession," *American Sociological Review*, 24, 4, August, 1959: 547-559.

[19] Beth Hartung, "The Plight of the Sociology Temporary." Pp. 269-288 in *A Critique of Contemporary American Sociology*, edited by T. Vaughn, G. Sjoberg and L. Reynolds. Dix Hills, NY: General Hall, 1993.

[20] Krier and Staples, *ibid.*

[21] Burris, *ibid.*

[22] John Flower, *Upstairs, Downstairs*. Akron, OH: University of Akron Press, 2004.

[23] *Ibid.*

[24] Michael Burawoy, "2004 American Sociological Association Presidential Address: For Public Sociology," *American Sociological Review*, 70, 1, February, 2005: 4-28.

[25] Craig Calhoun, "The Promise of Public Sociology," *British Journal of Sociology*, 56, 3, September, 2005: 355-363; Richard Ericson, "Publicizing Sociology," *British Journal of Sociology*, 56, 3, September, 2005: 365-372; John Scott, "Who Will Speak, and Who Will Listen? Comments on Burawoy and Public Sociology," *British Journal of Sociology*, 56, 3, September, 2005: 405-409; Wanda Katz-Fishman and John Scott, "Comments on Burawoy: A View from the Bottom Up," *Critical Sociology*, 31, 3, 2005: 371-374.

[26] Gregory Weiss and Dretha Phillips, "Participation of Sociologists at Two-Year and Four-Year Colleges in the American Sociological Association," *The American Sociologist*, 25, 3, Fall, 1994: 37-52.

[27] Lake Charles, LA, June 1, 2004.

[28] George Ritzer, *The McDonaldization of Society*. Thousand Oaks, CA: Pine Forge Press, 2004.

[29] *Ibid.*

[30] Based on interviews with faculty in Fort Worth, TX and Beaumont, TX.

[31] Gary Marx and Doug McAdam, *Collective Behavior and Social Movements*. Englewood Cliffs, NJ: Prentice Hall, 1994.

[32] Denton, TX, Summer, 1996.

[33] Lake Charles, LA, Spring, 2005.

[34] Lake Charles, LA, Summer, 2000.

[35] Houston, TX, Spring, 2005.

[36] Galveston, TX, Spring, 1994.

[37] Denton, TX, Spring, 2004; Denton, TX, Spring, 1997.

[38] Lake Charles, LA, Spring, 2003.

[39] Jerry Gaston, Herman Lantz and Charles R. Snyder, "Publication Criteria for Promotion in Ph.D. Graduate Departments," *The American Sociologist*, 10, November, 1975: 239-242.

[40] *Ibid.*

[41] Denton, TX, Spring, 1995.

[42] Tamotsu Shibutani, *Improvised News; A Sociological Study of Rumor*. Indianapolis, IN: Bobbs Merrill, 1966.

[43] George Kourvetaris to author, December 16, 2004.

[44] *Ibid.*

---

[45] Lake Charles, LA, Spring, 2002.

[46] Author to Kevin Leicht, Fall, 2002.

[47] Publisher to author, Spring, 2004.

[48] Joseph McFalls, Michael Engle, and Bernard Gallagher, "The American Sociologist: Characteristics in the 1990s," *The American Sociologist*, 30, 3, Fall, 1999: 96-100.

[49] Lake Charles, LA, Spring, 2003.

[50] Muzafer Sherif, *Social Judgment, Assimilation and Contrast Effects in Communication and Attitude Change.* New Haven, CT: Yale University Press, 1961.

[51] Ibid.

[52] Stanley Milgram, *Obedience to Authority: An Experimental View.* New York, NY: Harper and Row, 1975.

[53] Stanford Prison Experiment, www.prisonexp.org, opening page.

[54] *Ibid.*

[55] *Ibid*, Slide 5.

[56] *Ibid*, Slide 3

[57] *Ibid.*

[58] *Ibid*, Slide 4.

[59] *Ibid.*

[60] *Ibid*, Slide 5.

[61] *Ibid.* Slides 1-6.

[62] *Ibid*, Slides 7-8.

[63] *Ibid*, Slide 9.

[64] *Ibid.*

[65] *Ibid.*

[66] *Ibid*, Slide 10.

[67] *Ibid.*

[68] *Ibid*, Slide 11.

[69] *Ibid.*

[70] *Ibid*, Slide 12.

[71] *Ibid.*

[72] *Ibid*, Slide 13.

[73] *Ibid*, Slide 14.

[74] *Ibid*, Slide 15.

[75] *Ibid*, Slide 16.

[76] *Ibid*, Slide 17.

[77] *Ibid*, Slide 18.

[78] *Ibid.*

[79] *Ibid*, Slide 19.

[80] *Ibid.*

[81] *Ibid*, Slide 20.

[82] *Ibid.*

[83] *Ibid*, Slide 21.

[84] *Ibid.*

[85] *Ibid*, Slide 22.

[86] *Ibid.*

[87] *Ibid*, Slide 23.

[88] *Ibid*, Slide 24.

[89] *Ibid.*

[90] *Ibid*, Slide 25.

[91] *Ibid.*

[92] *Ibid*, Slide 27.

[93] *Ibid.*

[94] *Ibid*, Slide 28.

[95] *Ibid.*

[96] *Ibid*, Slide 29.

[97] *Ibid.*

[98] *Ibid*, Slide 30.

[99] *Ibid.*

[100] *Ibid*, Slide 31.

[101] *Ibid.*

[102] *Ibid.*

[103] *Ibid*, Slide 32.

[104] *Ibid*, Slide 33.

[105] *Ibid.*

[106] *Ibid*, Slide 34.

[107] *Ibid.*

[108] *Ibid*, Slide 35.

[109] *Ibid.*

[110] *Ibid.*

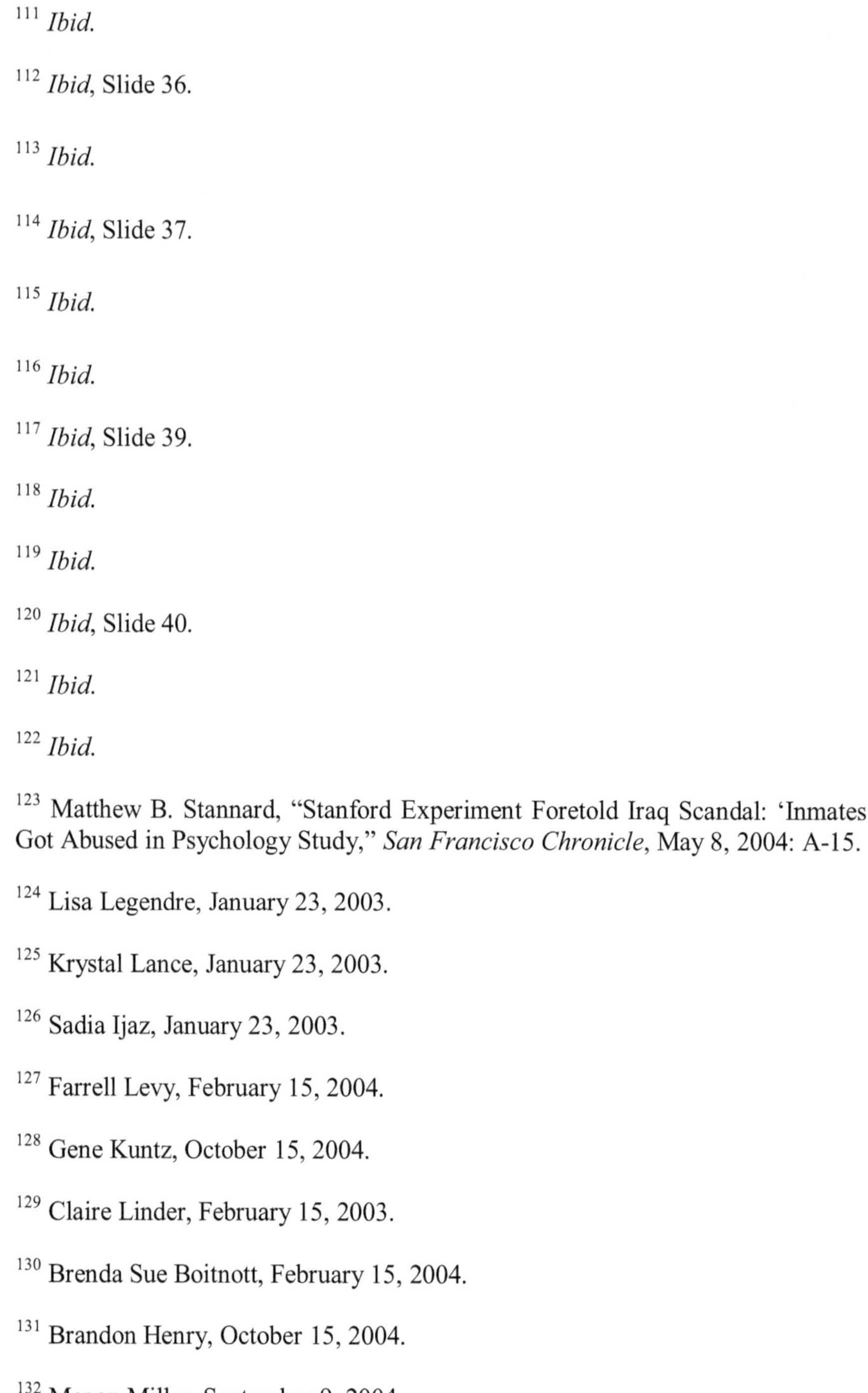

[111] *Ibid.*

[112] *Ibid*, Slide 36.

[113] *Ibid.*

[114] *Ibid*, Slide 37.

[115] *Ibid.*

[116] *Ibid.*

[117] *Ibid*, Slide 39.

[118] *Ibid.*

[119] *Ibid.*

[120] *Ibid*, Slide 40.

[121] *Ibid.*

[122] *Ibid.*

[123] Matthew B. Stannard, "Stanford Experiment Foretold Iraq Scandal: 'Inmates' Got Abused in Psychology Study," *San Francisco Chronicle*, May 8, 2004: A-15.

[124] Lisa Legendre, January 23, 2003.

[125] Krystal Lance, January 23, 2003.

[126] Sadia Ijaz, January 23, 2003.

[127] Farrell Levy, February 15, 2004.

[128] Gene Kuntz, October 15, 2004.

[129] Claire Linder, February 15, 2003.

[130] Brenda Sue Boitnott, February 15, 2004.

[131] Brandon Henry, October 15, 2004.

[132] Megan Miller, September 9, 2004.

[133] James Aho, *The Politics of Righteousness: Idaho Christian Patriotism.* Seattle: University of Washington Press, 1990; James Aho, *This Thing of Darkness: A Sociology of the Enemy.* Seattle: University of Washington Press, 1994; Sean O'Brien and Donald Haider-Markel, "Fueling the Fire: Social and Political Correlates of Citizen Militia Activity," *Social Science Quarterly*, 79, 1998: 456-465. While this research was originally in progress or in press, several quantitative studies emerged. See for example Joshua D. Freilich, *American Militias: State Level Variations in Militia Activity.* New York: LFB Scholarly Publishing, 2003; Nella Van Dyke and Sarah Soule, "Structural Social Change and the Mobilizing Effect of Threat: Explaining Level of Patriot and Militia Organizing in the United States," *Social Problems*, 49, 4, 2002: 497-520.

[134] Betty Dobratz and Stephanie Shanks-Meile, *White Power, White Pride? The White Separatist Movement in the United States.* New York: Prentice Hall International, 1997; Sara Diamond, *Roads to Dominion: Right Wing Movements and Political Power in the United States.* New York: Guilford Press, 1995; Jeffrey Kaplan and Tore Bjorno, *Nation and Race: The Developing Euro-American Racist Subculture.* Boston: Northeastern University Press, 1998; Jeffrey Kaplan and Leonard Weinberg, *Emergence of a Euro- American Radial Right.* New Brunswick: Rutgers University Press, 1998; Chip Berlet, *Eyes Right! Challenging the Right Wing Backlash.* Boston: South End Press, 1995; Chip Berlet and Matthew Lyons, *Right Wing Populism in America: Too Close for Comfort.* New York: Guilford Press, 2000.

[135] Billy Turner, "Domestic Terrorism." Pp. 498-501 in *Encyclopedia of Criminology and Deviant Behavior: Millennium Issue*, edited by Clifton Bryant. London: Francis and Taylor, 2001; Mark Hamm, *Terrorism, Hate Crime and Anti-Government Violence.* Washington, D.C.: National Research Council, 1996.

[136] John George and Laird Wilcox, *American Extremists: Militias, Supremacists, Klansmen, Communists, and Others*. Lanham: Prometheus Books, 1996.

[137] Dobratz and Shanks-Meile, *ibid.*

[138] Robert Merton, "Social Structure and Anomie," *American Sociological Review*, 3, 1938: 672-682.

[139] Neil Smelser, *Theory of Collective Behavior.* New York: Free Press of Glencoe, 1963.

[140] *Ibid.*

[141] Chip Berlet and Matthew Lyons, "Militia Nation," *Progressive*, 59, 1995: 22-25; Dan Junas, "The Rise of the Militias," Available online at: http://caq.com/caq/CAQ.militia.html (accessed on December 9, 1999).

[142] Charlotte Meador, "Fantasy Theme Chaining in Cyberspace: A Rhetorical Vision of the U.S. Militia Movement," Available online at: http://earthops.org/finale.html (accessed on December 17, 1999).

[143] Don Kates, "Handgun Prohibition and the Original Meaning of the Second Amendment," *Michigan Law_Review*, 82, 1983: 204-273; Stephen Halbrook, *That Every Man be Armed: The Evolution of a Constitutional Right*. Albuquerque: University of New Mexico Press, 1984.

[144] P. Salsich, "The Armed Superpatriots in the Midwest," *Nation*, November 11, 1961: 372-274.

[145] Aho, 1990, *ibid.*

[146] Harry Jones, *The Minutemen*. Garden City: Doubleday, 1968; Aho, 1990, *ibid*; James Corcoran, *Bitter Harvest*: *Gordon Kahl and the Posse Comitatus*. New York: Viking, 1991; Kevin Flynn and Gary Gerhardt, *The Silent Brotherhood*: *The Chilling Inside Story of America's Violent Antigovernment Militia Movement.* New York: Signet, 1995; George and Wilcox, *ibid.*

[147] Michael Barkun, *Religion and the Racist Right: The Origins of the Christian Identity Movement*. Chapel Hill: University of North Carolina Press, 1997.

[148] *Ibid.*

[149] State of California, Office of the Attorney General, *Paramilitary Organizations in California*. Sacramento: Office of the Attorney General, 1965.

[150] Barkun, *ibid*; Flynn and Gerhardt, *ibid.*

[151] William Pierce, *The Turner Diaries*. Washington, DC: National Alliance, 1978.

[152] Barkun, *ibid.*

[153] Aho, 1990, *ibid*; W. Mullins, "Hate Crime and the Far Right: Unconventional Terrorism." Pp. 121-169 in *Political Crime in Contemporary America*, edited by K. Tunnell. New York: Garland, 1993.

[154] Aho, 1994, *ibid*; David Helvarg, "The Anti-Enviro Connection," *Nation*, May 22, 1995: 722-724; Pat Robertson, *The New World Order*. Dallas: Word Publishing, 1991.

[155] Smelser, *ibid.*

[156] *Ibid.*

[157] *Ibid*; Talcott Parsons and Edward Shils, *Toward a General Theory of Action.* Cambridge: Harvard University Press, 1951.

[158] Smelser, *ibid.*

[159] *Ibid.*

[160] Leonard Weinberg, "The American Radical Right: Exit, Voice and Violence." Pp. 185-203 in *Encounters With the Contemporary Radical Right*, edited by P. Merkl and L. Weinberg. Boulder, CO: Westview Press, 1993.

[161] Berlet and Lyons, 1995, *ibid.*

[162] Smelser, *ibid.*

[163] Daniel Bell, *The Radical Right.* Garden City: Doubleday, 1963.

[164] Don McAlvany, *Toward a New World Order: The Countdown to Armageddon.* Oklahoma City: Hearthstone, 1990.

[165] Anthony Giddens, *Beyond Left and Right.* Palo Alto: Stanford University Press, 1994.

[166] Smelser, *ibid.*

[167] Kenneth Stern, *Militias, a Growing Danger.* New York: American Jewish Committee, 1995; *A Force Upon the Plain.* New York: Simon and Schuster, 1996.

[168] Mark Pitcavage, "Camouflage and Conspiracy: The Militia Movement from Ruby Ridge to Y2K," *American Behavioral Scientist*, 44, 6, 2001: 957-981; James Ridgeway and Leonard Zeskind, "Revolution USA," *Village Voice*, May 2, 1995: 23-26; U.S. Senate, *The Militia Movement in the United States: Hearings Before the Subcommittee on Terrorism, Technology and Government Information of the Committee on the Judiciary*. Washington: GPO, 1997.

[169] K. Schneider, "Fearing a Conspiracy, Some Heed a Call to Arms," *New York Times*, November 14, 1994: 1; Alexander Cockburn, "Beat the Devil," *Nation*, July 17, 1995: 80-81; R. McFadden, "Links in Blast: Armed 'Militia' and a Key Date," *New York Times*, April 22, 1995: 1.

[170] Barkun, 1997, *ibid*; Mark Hamm, *Apocalypse in Oklahoma: Waco and Ruby Ridge Revenged.* Boston: Northeastern University Press, 1997.

[171] Smelser, *ibid*; Max Weber, *The Theory of Social and Economic Organization.* Glencoe, IL: The Free Press, 1947.

[172] Smelser, *ibid.*

[173] Texas Militia Papers (TMP), Available online at: http://constitution.org/mil/tmp.htm, (accessed on July 15, 2000); Meador, *ibid.*

[174] Smelser, *ibid*; Southern Poverty Law Center (SPLC), *False Patriots: The Threat of Anti-Government Extremists.* Montgomery, AL: SPLC, 1996.

[175] Theda Skocpol and John Campbell, *American Society and Politics: Institutional, Historical, and Theoretical Perspectives.* New York: McGraw-Hill, 1995.

[176] James O'Connor, *The Fiscal Crisis of the State.* New York: St. Martin's Press, 1973.

[177] Robert Reich, *The Future of Success.* London: Heinemann, 2001.

[178] C. Keen, "UF Researcher: Militias are Armed, Dangerous - and Educated," Available online at: http://nuance.dhs.org/lbo-talk/9806/0583.html, (accessed on April 13, 2001); Robert Snow, *The Militia_Threat: Terrorists Among Us.* New York: Plenum Trade, 1999; Harvey Kushner, *Terrorism in America: A Structured Approach to Understanding the Terrorist Threat.* Springfield: Charles C. Thomas, 1998.

[179] Doug McAdam, *Political Process and the Development of Black Insurgency.* Chicago: University of Chicago Press, 1982.

[180] David Snow, E. Burke Rochford, Steven Worden, and Robert Benford, “Frame Alignment Processes, Micromobilization, and Movement Participation,” *American Sociological Review*, 51, 1986: 464-481; D. McAdam, J. McCarthy, and M. Zald, "Social Movements." Pp. 695-737 in *Handbook of Sociology*, edited by Neil Smelser. London: Sage, 1988.

[181] Earl Babbie, *The Practice of Social Research.* Belmont: Wadsworth, 1995.

[182] Stern, 1995, *ibid.*

[183] *Ibid*; George and Wilcox, *ibid*; Thomas Halpern and Brian Levin, *The Limits of Dissent: The Constitutional Status of Armed Citizen Militias.* Amherst: Aletheia Press, 1996; James Duffy and Alan Brantley, "Militias: Initiating Contact," Available online at: http://fbi.gov/library/leb/1997/July975.htm, (accessed on August 3, 2000).

[184] SPLC, 1996, *ibid*; SPLC, *Active Patriot Groups in the U.S. in 1996*. Montgomery, AL: SPLC, 1997; John Whitley, "New World Order Intelligence Update," Available online at: http://Home.InfoRamp.Net/~jwhitley/, (accessed on August 21, 1998).

[185] SPLC, *Active Patriot Groups in the U.S. in 1997*. Montgomery, AL: SPLC, 1998.

[186] SPCL, 1996, *ibid.*

[187] Chip Berlet, "Hard Right Conspiracism and Apocalyptic Millennialism," Available online at: http://www.publiceye.org/media/hardrit.html, (accessed on December 19, 2001).

[188] *Ibid.*

[189] Qualitative Data Solutions (QDS), *Nonnumerical Unstructured Data Indexing Searching and Theorizing*. Melbourne: Qualitative Solutions and Research, 1994.

[190] Berlet and Lyons, *ibid*; Junas, *ibid.*

[191] Stern, 1996, *ibid.*

[192] *Ibid.*

[193] Smelser, *ibid.*

[194] Meador, *ibid.*

[195] Smelser, *ibid.*

[196] SPLC, 1996, *ibid.*

[197] Berlet and Lyons, 1995, *ibid*; Ridgeway and Zeskind, *ibid.*

[198] Aho, 1996, *ibid.*

[199] Post 12.

[200] Post 238.

[201] Jonathan Karl, *The Right to Bear Arms: The Rise of America's New Militias*. New York: Harper Paperbacks, 1995; David Bennett, *The Party of Fear: From Nativist Movements to the New Right in American History*. New York: Vintage, 1995; Kushner, *ibid*; Snow, *ibid*; McAlvany, *ibid.*

[202] Post 104.

[203] Post 297.

[204] Post 11.

[205] Post 238.

[206] Karl, *ibid*; Snow, *ibid*; Stern, 1995, *ibid*; D. Hoffman, "America's Militias: Angry White Guys or Defenders of Liberty?" Available online at: http://www.webcom.com/haight/features/militia/white.html (accessed on December 27, 1999); Steve Macko, "The Aryan Republican Army," Available online at:
http://www.emergency.com/aryanarm.htm (accessed on December 9, 1999).

[207] Smelser, *ibid.*

[208] *Ibid.*

[209] Michael Barkun, "Militias, Christian Identity and the Radical Right," *Christian Century*, 112, 1995: 738; Jess Walter, *Every Knee Shall Bow: The Truth and Tragedy of Ruby Ridge and the Weaver Family*. New York: Harper Paperbacks, 1995; Karl, *ibid*; Halpern and Levin, *ibid*; Hamm, 1997, *ibid*; Kushner, *ibid*; Snow, *ibid.*

[210] Bennett, *ibid*; Mark Koernke, *America in Peril*. Topeka: Prophecy Club, 1993; Linda Thompson, *Waco,_the Big Lie*. Indianapolis: American Justice Federation, 1993.

[211] SPLC, 1996, *ibid.*

[212] George and Wilcox, *ibid.*

[213] Mike Kemp, "Now a Way to Expose Infiltrators," Available online at: http://www.link2000.net/~preacher/pat4prf1.htm (accessed on December 21, 1999).

[214] Louis Beam, "Leaderless Resistance," *Seditionist*, 12, 1992: 1-6.

[215] Post 31.

[216] Post 78.

[217] Bennett, *ibid*; Kushner, *ibid.*

[218] Stern, 1996, *ibid*; Martin Lindstedt, "Dangerous Liaisons," Available online at: http://www2.mo-net.com/~mlindste/mmmisu5.html (accessed on December 9, 1999).

[219] Seymour Lipset and Earl Raub, *The Politics of Unreason: Right-Wing Extremism in America, 1790-1977*. Chicago: University of Chicago Press, 1978.

[220] Verta Taylor, "Social Movement Continuity: The Women's Movement in Abeyance," *American Sociological Review*, 54, 1989: 761-775.

[221] Gordon Witkin, "The Secret FBI-Militia Alliance," *U.S. News and World Report*, May 12, 1997: 40-41.

[222] Giddens, *ibid.*

[223] David Snow and Robert Benford, "Ideology, Frame Resonance, and Participant Mobilization," *International Social Movement Research*, 1, 1988: 197-217.

[224] Centers For Disease Control and Prevention, "Guide to Prevent Tobacco Use and Addiction" (fact sheet), National Center For Chronic Disease and Health Promotion. Atlanta, GA: CDCP, 2002; American Heart Association, "Tobacco Industry's Targeting of Youth, Minorities, and Women" (fact sheet). Dallas, TX: AHA, 2003; G. Reza Najem, Fatima Batuman, Ann Marie Smith, and Martin Feuerman, "Patterns of Smoking Among Inner-City Teenagers: Smoking Has a Pediatric Age of Onset, *Journal of Adolescent Health*, 20, 3, 1997, pp. 226-231.

[225] U.S. Public Health Service, *Preventing Tobacco Use among Young People: A Report of the Surgeon General: At-a-Glance*. Rockville, MD: U.S. Department of Health and Human Services, Substance Abuse and Mental Health Services Administration, Center for Mental Health Services, 1994.

[226] Centers for Disease Control, 2002, *ibid*; National Institute on Drug Abuse, *Research Report Series –Nicotine Addiction*. Bethesda, MD: NIDA, 2002.

[227]U.S. Department of Health and Human Services, *National Household Survey on Drug Abuse: Main Finding, 1977*. Rockville, MD: HHS, 1999.

[228] L.L. Pederson, J.C. Baskerville, and N.M. Lefcoe, "Prevalence of and Factors Related to Cigarette Smoking Among Students in Grade 6," *Journal of Drug Education*, 13, 4, 1983: 305-312.

[229] Centers for Disease Control and Prevention, *Women and Smoking*. National Center For Chronic Disease and Health Promotion. Atlanta, GA: CDCP, 2001; William Latimer, Leah Floyd, Marco Vasquez, Megan O'Brien, Abigail Arzola, and Nancy Rivera, "Substance Use Among School-Based Youths in Puerto Rico:

Differences Between Gender and Grade Levels," *Addictive Behaviors*, 29, 8, November, 2001: 1659-1664.

[230] I. Sutherland and J.P. Shepherd, "Adolescents' Beliefs About Future Substance Use: A Comparison of Current Users and Non-Users of Cigarettes, Alcohol and Illicit Drugs," *Journal of Adolescence*, 25, 2, April, 2002: 169-181.

[231] Jayne Fulkerson and Simone French, "Cigarette Smoking for Weight Loss or Control Among Adolescents: Gender and Racial/Ethnic Differences," *Journal of Adolescent Health*, 32, 4, April, 2003: 306-313; Arthur Crisp, Phillip Sedgwick, Christine Halek, Neil Joughin, and Heather Humphrey, "Why May Many Teenage Girls Persist in Smoking?" *Journal of Adolescence*, 22, 5, October, 1999: 657-672.

[232] Elizabeth Goodman and John Capitman, "Depressive Symptoms and Cigarette Smoking Among Teens," *Pediatrics*, 106, 4, 2000: 748-755.

[233] James Kirby, "The Influence of Parental Separation on Smoking Initiation in Adolescents," *Journal of Health and Social Behavior*, 43, 1, March, 2002: 56-71.

[234] Alan Flisher, Charles Parry, Janet Evans, Martie Muller, and Carl Lombard, "Substance Use by Adolescents in Cape Town: Prevalence and Correlates," *Journal of Adolescent Health*, 32, 1, January, 2003: 58-65; Phillip Ritchey, Gerald Reid, and Lora Hasse, "The Relative Influence of Smoking on Drinking and Drinking on Smoking Among High School Students in a Rural Tobacco Growing County," *Journal of Adolescent Health*, 29, 6, December, 2001: 386-394; Patrick Miller, "Family Structure, Personality, Drinking, Smoking and Illicit Drug Use: A Study of UK Teenagers," *Drug and Alcohol Dependence*, 45, 1-2, April, 1997: 121-129.

[235] Diane Straub, Nancy Hills, Pamela Thompson, and Anna-Barbara Moscicki, "Effects of Pro and Anti Tobacco Advertising on Nonsmoking Adolescents' Intentions to Smoke," *Journal of Adolescent Health,* 32, 1, January, 2003: 36-43.

[236] Cynthia Pomerleau, "Co-Factors for Smoking and Evolutionary Psychobiology," *Addiction*, 92, 4, 1997: 397-408.

[237] Margareta Von Bothmer, B. Mattsson, and B. Fridlund, "Influences on Adolescent Smoking Behaviour: Siblings' Smoking and Norms in the Social Environment Do Matter," *Health and Social Care in the Community*, 10, 4, July, 2002: 213-220.

[238] Bruce Simons-Morton, "Prospective Analysis of Peer and Parent Influences on Smoking Initiation Among Early Adolescents," *Prevention Science*, 3, 4, 2002: 275; Alison Bryant, John Schulenberg, Patrick O'Malley, Jerald Bachman, and Lloyd Johnston, "How Academic Achievement, Attitudes and Behaviors Relate to

the Substance Use During Adolescence: A 6-Year, Multi-Wave National Longitudinal Study," *Journal of Research on Adolescence*, 13, 3, 2003: 361-397.

[239] Stacey Adamzyck-Robinette, Anne Fletcher, and Kristie Wright, "Understanding the Authoritative Parenting-Early Adolescent Tobacco Link: The Mediating Role of Peer Tobacco Use," *Journal of Youth and Adolescence*, 31, 4, August, 2002: 311-318.

[240] Von Bothmer *et al., ibid.*

[241] Jeffrey Arnett, "Adolescents' Responses to Cigarette Advertisements for Five 'Youth Brands' and One 'Adult Brand,'" *Journal of Research on Adolescence*, 11, 4, 2001: 425-443.

[242] Lynn MacFayden, Amanda Amos, Gerard Hastings, and Edward Parkes, "'They Look Like My Kind of People' – Perceptions of Smoking Images in Magazines," *Social Science and Medicine*, 56, 3, February, 2003: 491-499.

[243] Judith McCool, Linda Cameron, and Keith Petrie, "Adolescent Perceptions of Smoking Imagery in Film," *Social Science and Medicine*, 52, 10, May, 2001: 1577-1587.

[244] Juliet L. Hatcher and Juliet Scarpa, "Reducing Tobacco Use in Adolescents: What Works, What Doesn't," *NAADAC News*, 12, 4, 2002: 16.

[245] Stephen E. Gardner, Patricia F. Green, and Carol Marcus, (Eds.), *Signs of Effectiveness II: Preventing Alcohol, Tobacco, and Other Drug Use: A Risk Factor Resiliency-Based Approach*. Washington, D.C.: Center For Substance Abuse Prevention, 1994.

[246] Joel Fischer and Kevin Corcoran, *Measure of Clinical Practice: A Sourcebook*. Volume 1: Couples, Families, and Children. New York: Free Press, 1994; L. P. Lipsitt, "A Self-Concept Scale for Children and its Relationship to the Children's Form of the Manifest Anxiety Scale," *Child Development*, 29, 1958: 463-472.

[247] Fischer and Corcoran, *ibid*; P.P. Hirschfield, Response Set in Impulsive Children," *Journal of Genetic Psychology*, 107, 1965: 117-126.

[248] Fischer and Corcoran, *ibid*; J.R. Buri, "Self Esteem and Appraisals of Parental Behavior," *Journal of Adolescent Behavior*, 4, 1989: 33-49.

[249] Fischer and Corcoran, *ibid*; M. Rosenberg, *Conceiving the Self*. New York: Basic Books, 1979.

---

[250] K. Kobus, "Peers and Adolescent Smoking," *Addiction*, 98, Supplement 1, 2003: 37-55.

[251] C.S. Campbell and J.W. Robinson, "The Effects of Teens Offering Positive Support on Preadolescent Client's Attitude Toward the Use of Street Drugs, Alcohol, and Tobacco, and Their Choice of Peers." Lake Charles, LA: McNeese State University, 2001; C.S. Campbell and S.C. Weeber, "Annual Review of the TOPS Program." Lake Charles, LA: McNeese State University, 2002.

[252] See chapter 1 of this book.

[253] See chapter 1 of this book.

[254] Starkville, MS, Fall, 1975.

[255] See chapter 1.

[256] Denton, TX, Fall, 1998.

[257] Norma Williams, Denton, TX, Fall, 1994.

[258] Denton, TX, Fall, 1994.

[259] This is the "Matthew Effect"; see Zuckerman and Merton, *ibid.*

www.ingramcontent.com/pod-product-compliance
Lightning Source LLC
Chambersburg PA
CBHW060311290526
45789CB00001B/482

* 9 7 8 1 4 6 3 5 2 0 8 6 1 *